"This is a handy book wi~~~~~~~~~~~~~~~~~~~~~busy people."

"A refreshi~~~~~~~~~~~~~~~~~~~~~~~~~~~~~~~ok will equip you
to be 'alw~~~~~~~~~~~~~~~~~~~~~~~~~~~~s within you.'"

~~~~earts radio host

Outstanding...such good answers!"
CHUCK SMITH
founding pastor, Calvary Chapel Costa Mesa, California

"I hope many seekers will give serious consideration to the thoughts so
well expressed in this timely and pithy book. Well worth reading."
CHARLES COLSON
author and founder of Prison Fellowship

"Charlie is a man of integrity, a true Berean, and a personal encouragement to
me. I'm excited to see what the Lord has in store for this man of faith."
JEREMY CAMP
Dove Award winner

"The Christian faith is the most reasonable faith in the world, and Charlie Campbell
shows that in a straightforward and down-to-earth way in this book. I thoroughly
enjoyed reading it and plan to give it away to as many people as I can."
BRIAN BRODERSEN
associate pastor, Calvary Chapel Costa Mesa, California

"I would like to thank Charlie for *One-Minute Answers to Skeptics* and congratulate him as
well. It is both basic and excellent in that it provides simple, accurate, and precise answers
to many questions that people have in their struggles to understand the Bible. I appreciated
Charlie's ability to take the often difficult questions and answer them very well."
DON MCCLURE
pastor, author, and founder of Calvary Way Ministries

"*One-Minute Answers to Skeptics* is a much-needed book in the world today.
Charlie Campbell has done an excellent job bringing readers answers to age-old
questions. He has shed light in a dark world with this easy and enjoyable read."
MIKE MACINTOSH
founder and president, Horizon International Ministries

"In his book, Charlie Campbell invites every honest skeptic to take a good look
at the Christian worldview, if for no other reason than to be better informed as
to how the Bible answers man's most intriguing and challenging questions and
why Christianity is a reasonable faith. Succinctly written, *One-Minute Answers
to Skeptics* offers concise information for both skeptic and believer alike."
JACK HIBBS
pastor, Calvary Chapel Chino Hills, California

"I have heard that one definition of genius is taking complex things and being able to simplify them. I was impressed that such difficult questions could be adequately answered in such a few lines. I think the majority of Christians who want and need answers to tough questions like these often want a simple, sufficient answer without having to read an entire book on the subject. In quick, simple answers, Charlie has done it. I know this was not easy, but on behalf of Christians everywhere and in all sincerity, thanks."

BRYAN NEWBERRY
pastor, Calvary Chapel San Diego, California

"Succinctly and very powerfully answers skeptics' questions…
It is immensely readable…I highly recommend this book."

WILLIAM M. ALNOR
author, professor, and access director of the Spiritual Counterfeits Project

"Great primer for apologetics! *One-Minute Answers to Skeptics* strikes a great balance—crisp, well-structured responses that also whet the appetite for deeper study. Seekers, skeptics, and believers will all benefit from Charlie's clear presentation and readable style."

LLOYD PULLEY
pastor, Calvary Chapel Old Bridge, New Jersey

"Charlie Campbell has done a wonderful job of earnestly contending for the faith. His depth of thought will be a powerful tool for leaders and defenders of the faith, and his succinct clarity will be a blessing to all who want to know the truth."

BRITT MERRICK
senior pastor, Reality Carpinteria, California

"Charlie Campbell provides believers with one of the most useful tools to come along in a long time. In fact, I know of no other book that covers so much important territory in such a short time."

GEORGE BRYSON
author and missionary

"It is with tremendous excitement that I can wholeheartedly recommend this long anticipated work by Charlie Campbell."

CHUCK WOOLEY
pastor, The Bridge Calvary Chapel, Palm Springs, California

"Charlie Campbell has an incredible gift for simplifying that which can seem complicated. This book is a great example of that."

ROB SALVATO
pastor, Calvary Chapel Vista, California

"A simple answer that you can remember is more useful than a complex answer that you can't quite recall. *One-Minute Answers to Skeptics* provides answers you can give when on the spot."

CARL WESTERLUND
director of the School of Ministry, Calvary Chapel Costa Mesa, California

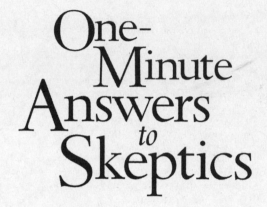

One-Minute Answers to Skeptics

CHARLIE H. CAMPBELL

HARVEST HOUSE PUBLISHERS
EUGENE, OREGON

ONE-MINUTE ANSWERS TO SKEPTICS

Copyright © 2005/2010 by Charlie H. Campbell
Published by Harvest House Publishers
Eugene, Oregon 97402
www.harvesthousepublishers.com

Library of Congress Cataloging-in-Publication Data

Campbell, Charlie H.
One-minute answers to skeptics / Charlie H. Campbell.
  p. cm.
Includes bibliographical references.
ISBN 978-0-7369-2918-9 (pbk.)
ISBN 978-0-7369-3714-9 (eBook)
1. Apologetics—Miscellanea. I. Title.
BT1103.C36 2010
239—dc22
                                                      2009029456

This book is dedicated to high school and college age people who are questioning the validity of the Christian faith, as well as to all those who desire to give a defense of the Christian faith to those who ask.

The truth shall make you free (JOHN 8:32).

Acknowledgments

I am indebted to the following men for their scholarly research and writings. They have shaped my thinking, strengthened my faith, and inspired me with ways to answer the kinds of questions I address in this book: Norman Geisler, William Lane Craig, Ravi Zacharias, J.P. Moreland, Ron Rhodes, Greg Koukl, Josh McDowell, Phillip E. Johnson, John Ankerberg, Lee Strobel, Charles Colson, John Walvoord, Henry Morris, Gary Habermas, Dave Hunt, Don Stewart, Ken Ham, Ron Carlson, Ray Comfort, Dan Story, and C.S. Lewis.

Thank you, Gene Skinner, Karen Robbins, Ron and Cindy Barger, MaryAnne Hommel, and Steve Erenyi for the hours you spent editing the manuscript of this book and for your invaluable suggestions.

Thank you, Calvary Chapel Vista, California, and especially Rob Nash and Bill Wright, for your ongoing help, encouragement, love, and prayers.

Thank you Anastasia, Selah, Addison, Caden, and Emerie, my wonderful family, for your undying, amazing love and support. You are my greatest treasures.

My deepest gratitude is reserved for You, Jesus, my Friend, Shepherd, Savior, and King. Thank You for rescuing me from my unbelief and sin in 1990. It is a joy, too deep for words, to know You and serve You. It is for You that I live and breathe.

Contents

1. "What evidence do you have that there is a God?"

2. "What evidence do you have that the Bible is actually true?"

3. "Hasn't the Bible undergone corruption as it was translated hundreds of times down through the centuries?"

4. "What about those who have never heard of Jesus? Will they be condemned to hell?"

5. "If God is so loving, why does He allow evil and suffering?"

6. "How do you know Jesus even existed?"

7. "How can you say Jesus is the only way to heaven?"

8. "Wasn't the deity of Christ an invention by the church during the fourth century at the Council of Nicea?"

9. "Doesn't it seem unfair and narrow that God would save people only through Jesus?"

10. "How can a loving God send somebody to hell?"

11. "Haven't certain books of the Bible been lost?"

12. "Isn't there a conflict between the God of the Old Testament, who is often portrayed as cruel, and the God of the New Testament, who seems very loving?"

13. "Why do many Protestants reject the apocryphal writings in the Catholic Bible?"

14. "Doesn't the Bible have a bunch of contradictions in it?"

15. "Wasn't the New Testament written down hundreds of years after Jesus lived? Wouldn't that make it unreliable?"

16. "Doesn't the Bible have scientific errors in it?"

17. "How do you know that Christianity is true and not some other religion, like Buddhism or Islam?"

18. "What about homosexuals? Do you believe they go to hell?"

19. "How can you be sure Jesus rose from the dead?"

20. "What about evolution? Haven't Darwin's theories disproved God's existence?"

21. "If everything needs a maker, as Christians seem to suggest, who made God?"

22. "If God doesn't need a maker, why couldn't we just say the universe doesn't need a maker either?"

23. "Can God make a rock so big He cannot move it? Yes or No?"

24. "How (or where) did Cain get his wife?"

25. "How can you adhere to a religion that would advocate such events as the Crusades?"

26. "What about the Old Testament, where Joshua and the nation of Israel were commanded by God to go through the land of Canaan and destroy everyone? How can you believe in a God who would command such a thing?"

Are You a Skeptic?

Do you have questions or doubts about the existence of God? Do you wonder if what the Bible says is really true? Do you question why God would allow evil and suffering? If so, I can relate. Those are the kinds of questions I used to have. Although I was raised in a Christian home, the faith I had as a child eroded into agnosticism and eventually atheism some time after junior high school. It was not until 1990, when I received intellectually satisfying answers to my questions, that my faith in God was slowly resurrected.

Skepticism regarding matters of the Christian faith is, of course, nothing new. The Bible itself mentions many people who were skeptics or who had questions and doubts about such matters. The people in Capernaum, on the shore of the Sea of Galilee, wanted to have evidence before they would believe. They asked Jesus, "What sign will You perform then, that we may see it and believe You? What work will You do?" (John 6:30).

The imprisoned and apparently doubting John the Baptist, whose faith had at one time been so strong, sent two messengers to ask Jesus, "Are You the Coming One, or do we look for another?" (Luke 7:19).

Thomas, one of the original 12 disciples, was skeptical of Jesus' resurrection, and said, "Unless I see in His hands the print of the nails, and put my finger into the print of the nails, and put my hand into His side, I will not believe" (John 20:25).

Pontius Pilate questioned Jesus about who He was and then finally asked, "What is truth?" (John 18:38).

We could add to this list the two disciples leaving Jerusalem after Jesus' crucifixion (Luke 24:13) and others.

How did Jesus respond to these people who had honest doubts and questions? Did He condemn them? Did He exhort them to put away their questions, suppress their doubts, and simply believe? No. Jesus lovingly and graciously gave them answers. He gave them evidence.

To John the Baptist, Jesus sent two messengers to tell of all the miraculous things He had just done (Luke 7:21-23). To doubting Thomas, Jesus showed Himself alive after His crucifixion and allowed Thomas to see the wounds in His hands and His side (John 20:26-29). For the discouraged disciples leaving Jerusalem, who were convinced that Jesus' death disproved any claim He had to be the Messiah, Jesus met them after His resurrection and showed them that the Scriptures had prophesied long beforehand that the Messiah was going to suffer (Luke 24:13-27). The Bible tells us that Jesus gave "many convincing proofs" (Acts 1:3 NASB).

The God of the Bible does not require that we blindly follow Him.

- The Bible tells us to "examine everything carefully" and to believe only that which is actually true (1 Thessalonians 5:21 NASB; see also Colossians 2:4).

- The Bible commends the people in the city of Berea for verifying that the words spoken by the apostle Paul were actually true (Acts 17:11).

- God desires that we use our minds and not just our hearts (Matthew 22:37).

- God says, "Come now, and let us reason together" (Isaiah 1:18).

- The Bible exhorts Christians to have answers for people with questions (1 Peter 3:15).

- God desires all people "to come to the knowledge of the truth" (1 Timothy 2:4).

Why does God want to reason with you? Why does He want you to come to the knowledge of the truth? Why does He want Christians to have answers for you? He loves you and wants to have a relationship with you (John 3:16). He wants you to experience the joy and wonder of knowing Him and His Son, Jesus Christ, not only in this life but also in eternity. Have your unanswered questions regarding Christianity kept you from knowing God? My hope and prayer for you is that this book will help answer your questions. Ultimately, my prayer is that you will come to realize and experience the joy of having a relationship with Jesus. He truly is the Son of God. He came to this earth two thousand years ago, died on the cross for your sins, and rose again so that you might experience God's forgiveness and everlasting life.

If the short answers in this book do not sufficiently lay to rest your doubts, I urge you to pick up one of these books:

Reasonable Faith: Christian Truth and Apologetics by William Lane Craig

I Don't Have Enough Faith to Be an Atheist by Norman Geisler and Frank Turek

Answering the Objections of Atheists, Agnostics, and Skeptics by Ron Rhodes

The Case for Faith by Lee Strobel

These books and the others I mention in the notes provide in-depth discussions of many of the issues addressed in this book. If you desire to know God in a personal way, please see "Steps to Peace with God" on page 99.

May God bless you and guide you into the truth.

Introduction

Always be ready to give a defense.

1 PETER 3:15

I was eating lunch at a restaurant with a friend a while back when our waitress saw our opened Bibles on the table. I am always amazed at the conversations that ensue after someone sees an open Bible. Doing a double take at the open Bibles, she asked, "Are you guys Christians or something?" We said yes and asked her if she had any spiritual beliefs.[1] She said she used to be a Christian but had changed her views a few years ago while she was taking a philosophy class at a local college. She went on to tell us that she now believed all roads lead to heaven. We talked with her for a moment about Jesus' exclusive claims regarding salvation in John 14:6 ("I am the way, the truth, and the life. No one comes to the Father except through Me") and the fact that He proved that what He was saying was true by His resurrection from the dead. She listened intently and then had to get back to work.

As ambassadors for Christ (2 Corinthians 5:20), we need

to be prepared (1 Peter 3:15; Jude 3) for open doors to speak of Christ and share the truth. The doors are often only open for a minute, and then they are shut.

What follows in this book are examples of ways you can answer a variety of questions in less than a minute. When someone asks me, "What evidence do you have that the Bible is actually true?" I do not attempt to walk them through a whole pile of evidence ("The *eighth* reason is…"). I try to answer their question in less than a minute or two. Frankly, that is all the time people often have before their cell phone rings, the baby starts crying, or they have to get back to work. If they want to hear a more in-depth response to their question, I let them know that I would be glad to go on.

The questions I have compiled (in no particular order) are 40 of the most common questions unbelievers and skeptics pose to Christians about God, the Bible, hell, salvation, and so on. I do not mean to imply by the title of the book that these are the most challenging or difficult questions that skeptics could ask, only that these are, in my opinion, 40 of the most popular questions they do ask. My prayer for you, if you are already a Christian, is that your faith will be strengthened and you will be better equipped to answer these questions the next time they come up in your own life.

May God bless this book for His glory, the strengthening of the saints, and the furtherance of the gospel.

Charlie H. Campbell
September 2005

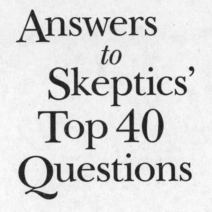

Answers
to
Skeptics'
Top 40
Questions

On the Universe:

"A proponent of the big bang theory, at least if he is an atheist, must believe that the matter of the universe came from nothing and by nothing."

> Anthony Kenny (1931–), author and former pro-vice-chancellor of the University of Oxford and president of the British Academy. *The Five Ways: St. Thomas Aquinas' Proofs of God's Existence* (Routledge, 1969), p. 66.

"When you realize that the laws of nature must be incredibly finely tuned to produce the universe we see, that conspires to plant the idea that the universe did not just happen, but that there must be a purpose behind it."

> John Polkinghorne (1930–), author, former physicist and professor, and winner of the Templeton Prize. "Science Finds God," *Newsweek*, July 20, 1998.

1. "What evidence do you have that there is a God?"

The very existence of the universe itself is evidence that there is a God. Let's think about this for a moment. There are only three options for the existence of the universe. One is that it has always been. Another is that it came into being by itself. The third is that it was created.

The first option, that the universe is eternal, has been utterly rejected by the scientific community. The motion of the galaxies, the background radiation echo, and other evidences all overwhelmingly point to the fact that the universe sprang into existence at a particular point in time, something scientists call the Big Bang.

The second option, that the universe created itself, is philosophically impossible. Of course, before the universe existed it would not have been around to do the creating. Obviously, a nonexistent universe could not have done anything! It did not exist. We all know that nothing cannot do anything. Nothing is nothing. It (if we could even call nothing an it!) cannot see, smell, act, think, or create. So option one and two can be thrown out on scientific and philosophical grounds.

The third option, that something or someone outside of the universe created the universe, is the only reasonable option.

Let's imagine I am holding up a painting. When you see a painting, what proof do you need to establish the fact that a painter exists? Nothing besides the painting itself. The painting is absolute proof that there was a painter. You do not need to see the painter to believe that he or she exists. The painting is all the evidence you need. It would not be there if the painter did not exist, and so it is with the universe. The existence of the universe itself proves absolutely that there is a creator.[2]

On Atheism:

"I am persuaded that men think there is no God because they wish there were none. They find it hard to believe in God, and to go on in sin, so they try to get an easy conscience by denying His existence."

Charles H. Spurgeon (1834–1892), British preacher and author.

2. "What evidence do you have that the Bible is actually true?"

If I had to answer this question with just a few evidences, I would probably mention fulfilled prophecies, archaeological discoveries, and the Bible's amazing unity.

The Bible, unlike any other religious book, has demonstrated itself to be the Word of God through its ability to rightly predict the future. There are literally hundreds of very specific prophecies in the Bible that were fulfilled hundreds of years after they were spoken.[3] No other religious book can verify itself in this way.

The Bible has also been proven to be historically reliable by numerous archaeological discoveries. To date, more than 25,000 archaeological discoveries have verified the names of persons, places, events, and customs mentioned in the Bible.

Finally, the Bible's unity is amazing. Here is a book that is actually a collection of 66 different books written down by more than 40 different authors over a period of more than 1500 years on three different continents and in three different languages. It addresses life's most controversial topics from beginning to end. You might expect to find chaos, confusion, and contradictions, yet the Bible miraculously remains absolutely consistent and internally harmonious from beginning to end.[4]

These three evidences (fulfilled prophecy, archaeological discoveries, and the Bible's amazing unity) build a compelling case for the divine origin and historical reliability of the Bible.[5]

On Archaeology:

"Archaeological work has unquestionably strengthened confidence in the reliability of the Scriptural record. More than one archaeologist has found his respect for the Bible increased by the experience of excavation in Palestine."

Millar Burrows (1889–1980), author and professor. *What Mean These Stones?* (American Schools of Oriental Research, 1941), p. 1.

3. "Hasn't the Bible undergone corruption as it was translated hundreds of times down through the centuries?"

The Bible has been translated into hundreds of different languages down through the centuries. You are right about that, but the text of the Bible has been accurately preserved all the way through. How do we know that to be the case?

First, we have plenty of manuscript evidence, including several thousand partial or complete ancient handwritten manuscript copies of the Bible, some dating as far back as the third century BC.[6] These manuscripts have allowed textual critics and scholars to verify that the Bible we have today is the same Bible the early church had.

Second, we also have the writings of the church fathers. By church fathers, I am referring to leaders in the early church.[7] In their commentaries on the Bible, their letters to one another, and their letters to other churches, these men quoted the New

Testament Scriptures alone more than 86,000 times. Their quotations have allowed scholars to reconstruct 99.86 percent of the New Testament. There are only 11 verses in the New Testament that the church fathers apparently never cited.

These two evidences, the manuscript evidence and the writings of the church fathers, verify conclusively that the original text of the Bible has been accurately preserved.[8]

On the Bible:

"The last foundation for any doubt that the Scriptures have come down to us substantially as they were written has now been removed. Both the authenticity and the general integrity of the books of the New Testament may be regarded as finally established."

Sir Frederic Kenyon (1863–1952), former director and principal librarian of the British Museum. *The Bible and Archaeology* (Harper & Brothers, 1940), pp. 288-89.

4.
"What about those who have never heard of Jesus? Will they be condemned to hell?"

The Bible says that God is merciful, gracious (Psalm 103:8) and loving (1 John 4:10) and that He is not willing that any should perish (2 Peter 3:9). The Bible also says that God is going to judge with righteousness and equity (Psalm 98:9). If people have not heard about Jesus, He will judge them based on what they do know through the testimony of creation and their conscience (Romans 1:20; 2:12-15).

The Bible says that "God is a rewarder of those who diligently seek Him" (Hebrews 11:6). There are many ways God can get the truth about salvation to those who truly seek to know Him. He can use a missionary (Acts 10), a radio broadcast, or a Bible (Psalm 119:130). Theoretically, God could send a vision (Daniel

2) or an angel (Revelation 14:6). The important thing for you to consider is that you *have* heard the truth. You have heard of Jesus' death on the cross for your sins, and God will hold you accountable for what you do with that information.[9]

On Science:

"It was my science that drove me to the conclusion that the world is much more complicated than can be explained by science. It is only through the supernatural that I can understand the mystery of existence."

Allan Sandage (1926–), award-winning American astronomer. "Science Finds God," *Newsweek*, July 20, 1998.

"Many have a feeling that somehow intelligence must have been involved in the laws of the universe...I strongly sense the presence and actions of a creative being far beyond myself and yet always personal and close by."

Charles Townes (1915–), physicist, author, and professor who shared the 1964 Nobel Prize in Physics for inventing the laser. "Science Finds God," *Newsweek*, July 20, 1998.

5. "If God is so loving, why does He allow evil and suffering?"

This is the most common question people have regarding God. Here is an interesting question for you to consider. What do you propose God should do about it? To stop evil and suffering, God would have to stop every act that causes any suffering. To do that, He would have to stop those who cause the suffering (adulterers, liars, murderers, criminals, fornicators, and so on). Wouldn't that mean He would have to put a stop to you and me too? Haven't we, by our own actions, caused some of the suffering that exists in the world? Haven't we hurt people's feelings? My friend, God has not destroyed evil because He would have to destroy us. By permitting evil and suffering to continue, God is actually showing the world mercy.

The Bible says that a day is coming when God will stop evil (2 Peter 3:7-13). He will judge sinners, put them away forever, and create a new heaven and a new earth, where there will no longer be any death, mourning, crying, or pain (Revelation 21:4). In the meantime, God is using the suffering that exists for good (Romans 8:28; Philippians 1:12). Often, when people are suffering, they turn to God and receive the kind of help they truly need.

On Suffering:

"God whispers to us in our pleasures, speaks in our conscience, but shouts in our pains: it is His megaphone to rouse a deaf world."

C.S. Lewis (1898–1963), author and professor. *The Problem of Pain* (MacMillan, 1962), p. 93.

"Supposing you eliminated suffering, what a dreadful place the world would be! I would almost rather eliminate happiness. The world would be the most ghastly place because everything that corrects the tendency of this unspeakable little creature, man, to feel over-important and over-pleased with himself would disappear. He's bad enough now, but he would be absolutely intolerable if he never suffered."

Malcolm Muggeridge (1903–1990), British author and journalist. *Jesus Rediscovered* (Doubleday, 1969), pp. 199-200.

6. "How do you know Jesus even existed?"

Of course, the New Testament, which has proven to be a reliable historical record, attests to Jesus' life. On top of that, at least 39 sources outside of the Bible attest to more than a hundred facts regarding Jesus' life, teachings, crucifixion, and resurrection.[10] For example, Flavius Josephus, a first-century Jewish historian, affirms not only that Jesus lived but also that He was "a doer of amazing deeds," that "Pilate condemned Him to be crucified to die," that He was a teacher who "won over many Jews and many of the Greeks," and that He was reportedly seen alive by His disciples after His crucifixion.[11]

The Babylonian Talmud is a collection of ancient Jewish writings. This extrabiblical source also mentions Jesus, even saying that He was killed on the eve of Passover, just as the biblical account describes.[12] Other noncanonical sources include the

Roman historian Tacitus, the Didache, Pliny the Younger, Suetonius, and the Gnostic Gospels (such as the Gospel of Thomas). The *Encyclopedia Britannica,* fifteenth edition, devotes 20,000 words to the person of Jesus Christ and never once hints that He didn't exist. The evidence is certain. Jesus of Nazareth was a real person.[13]

On Jesus:

"At this time there was a wise man who was called Jesus. And His conduct was good, and He was known to be virtuous. And many people from among the Jews and the other nations became His disciples. Pilate condemned Him to be crucified to die. And those who had become His disciples did not abandon His discipleship. They reported that He had appeared to them three days after His crucifixion and that He was alive."

Flavius Josephus (AD 37–c. 100), first-century Roman historian. *The Antiquities of the Jews,* 18:3.

7. "How can you say Jesus is the only way to heaven?"

That is what the Bible teaches.[14] Let's imagine for a moment that you have just hurt my feelings in a terrible way. You said and did some really mean things to me. Would you be able to go to just anyone and apologize to them in order to make *our* relationship right? Of course not. The same is true in our relationship with God. Mankind has sinned against God by the things we have said and done.[15] Therefore, to have our relationship restored, we must go back to Him, not to Buddha, Allah, Krishna, or some other imaginary, man-made deity. A person must go to Jesus and through Jesus because He is God. He is not a city, like Rome, of which it might be said, "All roads lead to Rome."

God is a personal being who has provided the gift of salvation (Romans 6:23) to all who will put their trust in His

Son, Jesus. If people put their faith in another savior (such as Buddha, Brahman, or Allah), they will find on judgment day that their god has done nothing for their eternal well-being, because their "so-called god" (1 Corinthians 8:5) does not exist (Isaiah 43:11; 45:5).

On God:

"To look out at this kind of creation and not believe in God is to me impossible."

John Glenn (1921–), astronaut and U.S. senator, as he looked out of the space shuttle *Discovery*, November 4, 1998. Quoted in Chuck Colson, "Astronauts Who Found God," *BreakPoint*, November 5, 1998.

"God's nature is revealed most perfectly in the life and teachings of Jesus of Nazareth, as recorded in the New Testament of the Bible, who was sent by God to reveal the divine nature."

George F.R. Ellis (1939–), theoretical cosmologist, professor, author, and recipient of the Templeton Prize. Nancey Murphey, et al., eds., *Quantum Cosmology and the Laws of Nature* (University of Notre Dame Press, 1997).

8. "Wasn't the deity of Christ an invention by the church during the fourth century at the Council of Nicea?"

Not at all.[16] The deity of Christ was mentioned in the Old Testament era more than 600 years before Jesus was born. Isaiah the prophet foretold that the Messiah would be called "Mighty God" in Isaiah 9:6. That certainly proved true.

The New Testament, which was completed in the first century, long before the Council of Nicea, is full of affirmations of Christ's deity.[17] For instance, Thomas called Jesus, "My Lord and my God!" (John 20:28). Paul called Jesus, "our great God and Savior Jesus Christ" (Titus 2:13). John called Jesus "God" in the opening verse of his Gospel (John 1:1). Jesus applied the name of God used in the Old Testament, "I AM" (Exodus 3:14), to Himself in John 8:58. He also said that God was His Father, resulting in some of His listeners trying to stone Him for making Himself "equal with God" (John 5:18; 10:33).

The second-century writings of church fathers, like Ignatius, Polycarp, Justin Martyr, Irenaeus, and Clement of Alexandria, also contain many references to Christ's deity.[18]

The resolution passed at the Council of Nicea in AD 325 was a reaffirmation of what the church at large already believed.

On Jesus:

"A man who was merely a man and said the sort of things Jesus said would not be a great moral teacher. He would either be a lunatic—on the level with the man who says he is a poached egg—or else he would be the Devil of Hell. You must make your choice. Either this man was, and is, the Son of God: or else a madman or something worse. You can shut Him up for a fool, you can spit at Him and kill Him as a demon; or you can fall at His feet and call Him Lord and God. But let us not come with any patronizing nonsense about His being a great human teacher. He has not left that open to us. He did not intend to."

C.S. Lewis (1898–1963), professor and author. *Mere Christianity* (MacMillan, 1960), pp. 40-41.

9. "Doesn't it seem unfair and narrow that God would save people only through Jesus?"

I do not see it that way. I think the question we should be asking is, "Why would God seek to save us at all?" When I consider my own sinfulness and the rampant rebellion and sinfulness that exists in the world today, I find it absolutely amazing that God has offered to save us at all!

Far from being narrow or unfair, God's offer of salvation is very gracious and broad. The Bible says that God loves the whole world (John 3:16; Romans 5:8), that Jesus died for the sins of all mankind (1 John 2:2), and that God is making salvation available to people on every continent. The gospel message is not just for Americans or Europeans or some other people group. Jesus told His disciples to take the good news "even to the remotest part of the earth" (Acts 1:8 NASB). The book of Revelation tells us that heaven will be populated with people "from every nation and all tribes and peoples and tongues" (Revelation 7:9 NASB). God's offer of salvation is broad and gracious.

On the Resurrection:

"If Jesus remained dead, how can you explain the reality of the Christian church and its phenomenal growth in the first three centuries of the Christian era? Christ's church covered the Western world by the fourth century. A religious movement built on a lie could not have accomplished that...All the power of Rome and of the religious establishment in Jerusalem was geared to stop the Christian faith. All they had to do was to dig up the grave and to present the corpse. They didn't."

Henry Schaefer III (1944–), professor and Nobel Prize nominee. "Questions Intellectuals Ask About Christianity," www.leaderu.com/offices /schaefer/docs/questions.html.

10. "How can a loving God send somebody to hell?"

The last thing God wants is for anyone to end up in hell. The Bible says that God is "not willing that any should perish" (2 Peter 3:9) and that He "desires all men to be saved and to come to the knowledge of the truth" (1 Timothy 2:4). God did more than simply proclaim His desire that none should perish. He actually *proved* His desire to save people when He left the glories of heaven in the person of Jesus and came to earth to die on the cross for our sins (John 3:16; Romans 5:8). Having paid the penalty for mankind's rebellion, God now graciously offers forgiveness and everlasting life as a gift (Romans 6:23) to all who will put their trust in Jesus.

If people reject God's grace; turn away from the testimony of their own conscience (Romans 2:15), the testimony of creation (Psalm 19:1-6; Acts 14:16-17), and the wooing of the Holy Spirit

(John 16:8); and say, "I will have nothing to do with God," God will, in the end, allow them to have their wish (2 Thessalonians 1:9). As C.S. Lewis said, "The damned are, in one sense, successful, rebels to the end...the doors of hell are locked on the inside."[19] In the end, those people who end up in hell will have only themselves to blame. Hell is the end of a path that is chosen to some degree in this life, here and now, day by day.[20]

Thy Will Be Done:

"There are only two kinds of people in the end: those who say to God, 'Thy will be done,' and those to whom God says, in the end, '*Thy* will be done.'"

C.S. Lewis (1898–1963), professor and author. *The Great Divorce* (Mac-Millan, 1946), p. 72.

11. "Haven't certain books of the Bible been lost?"

No. The supposedly lost books of the Bible that have been found, the so-called gospels of Thomas, Philip, and Mary Magdalene, were not lost gospels; they were pseudo gospels that the early church rejected as uninspired, spurious writings. The Christian church was familiar with these documents but purposely left them out of the Bible, easily recognizing that they were not divinely inspired.

We too can be certain these books do not belong in the Bible. First, they were not written by any of the apostles or their close associates (such as Mark or Luke). Most scholars, Christian and non-Christian, date these Gnostic gospels to the second and third centuries, long after the time of Christ. Secondly, these writings contradict authentic revelation.[21]

You can be absolutely confident that God, who inspired

the men to pen the words of the Bible (2 Timothy 3:16; 2 Peter 1:21), saw to it that none of the inspired writings were lost. We would be foolish to think that an all-knowing, all-powerful God could lose track of books He intended to put in the Bible (or anything else for that matter).

On the Bible:

"I must say, that having for many years made the evidences of Christianity the subject of close study, the result has been a firm and increasing conviction of the authenticity and plenary inspiration of the Bible. It is indeed the Word of God."

Simon Greenleaf (1783–1853), professor and founder of Harvard Law School. Correspondence with the American Bible Society, November 6, 1852.

"For eighteen centuries every engine of destruction that human science, philosophy, wit, reasoning or brutality could bring to bear against a book has been brought to bear against that book to stamp it out of the world, but it has a mightier hold on the world today than ever before. If that were man's book it would have been annihilated and forgotten hundreds of years ago."

R.A. Torrey (1856–1928), author and dean of the Bible Institute of Los Angeles. Charles Leach and R.A. Torrey, *Our Bible: How We Got It and Ten Reasons Why I Believe the Bible Is the Word of God* (The Bible Institute Colportage Association, 1898).

12.

"Isn't there a conflict between the God of the Old Testament, who is often portrayed as cruel, and the God of the New Testament, who seems very loving?"

Not at all. The God of the Old Testament is the very same loving God spoken of in the New Testament. The Old Testament says He is "gracious and merciful; slow to anger and great in lovingkindness" (Psalm 145:8 NASB). God says in Malachi 3:6, "I am the LORD, I do not change."

The Old Testament does contain more stories of God's judgment against sinners than does the New Testament (including the flood and the destruction of Sodom and Gomorrah). Keep in mind, though, that the Old Testament covers about four thousand years of history, and the New Testament covers less than a hundred years.

The God spoken of in the New Testament is just as serious about sin as He was in the Old Testament. The New Testament tells of a time when God's judgment is going to come upon the whole earth in the last days (Matthew 24:21; 2 Peter 3:7; Revelation 6–18). Beyond that, the New Testament clearly talks about a time when unrepentant, unforgiven sinners will stand before God to be judged for their sins (Revelation 20:12-15).

On the Bible:

"I have a fundamental belief in the Bible as the Word of God, written by men who were inspired. I study the Bible daily."

Sir Isaac Newton (1642–1727), physicist, mathematician, astronomer, inventor, philosopher, and alchemist. Quote cited at BlueLetterBible .org.

On Evolution:

"In grammar school they taught me that a frog turning into a prince was a fairy tale. In the university they taught me that a frog turning into a prince was a fact."

Ron Carlson, Christian apologist. Cited in Dr. Norman Geisler and Frank Turek, *I Don't Have Enough Faith to Be an Atheist* (Crossway, 2004), p. 137.

13. "Why do many Protestants reject the apocryphal writings in the Catholic Bible?"

There are numerous reasons why many Christians (including the early church) have rejected the apocryphal books as authoritative or divinely inspired. Let me share with you four reasons.[22]

First, the apocryphal writings contain numerous teachings that contradict authentic Scripture (including the practice of praying for the dead, the doctrine of purgatory, and the teaching that salvation is available through good works and the giving of alms). Second, the apocryphal writings contain numerous historical, geographical, and chronological errors.[23] Third, Jesus and the apostles cite the Old Testament nearly 300 times in the pages of the New Testament (referring to it as Scripture), but they never quote any of the apocryphal books accepted by the Roman Catholic Church.[24] Fourth, the apocryphal writings were never included in the Hebrew Bible. The Jews themselves, from whom the apocryphal writings came, did not accept the writings as divinely inspired. The apocryphal writings were not formally declared to be authoritative and inspired by the Catholic Church until the Council of Trent in AD 1546. The Catholic Church's acceptance of these writings into the canon of Scripture was an effort to counter the teachings of Martin Luther and the other leaders of the Reformation. These men were pointing out that many teachings of the Catholic Church came from the Apocrypha, not the 66 books of the Bible.

On the Authority of the Scriptures:

"Unless I am convinced by Scripture and plain reason—I do not accept the authority of the popes and councils, for they have contradicted each other—my conscience is captive to the Word of God. I cannot and I will not recant anything, for to go against conscience is neither right nor safe. Here I stand. I can do no other. God help me. Amen."

Martin Luther (1483–1546), German priest and scholar whose attempts to reform the Catholic Church led to the Protestant Reformation. He spoke these words at his trial at the Diet of Worms, April 18, 1521.

14. "Doesn't the Bible have a bunch of contradictions in it?"

No. Some verses in the Bible seem to contradict one another, but with a little investigation into the original languages, the context of the various passages, and the cultural and geographical settings in which the Bible was originally written, they are easily reconciled. Here is an example.

Luke 18:35 says that Jesus healed a blind man "as He was coming near Jericho." Mark 10:46 says Jesus healed the man "as He went out of Jericho." Critics contend that either Luke or Mark must have made a mistake. That does appear to be the case. What is the solution?

A German archaeologist named Ernst Sellin, working on an excavation in Israel between 1907 and 1909, discovered what have been called the twin cities of Jericho. One was the old Hebrew city, and the other was a newer Roman city. The two cities, both called Jericho, were separated from one another by about a mile. Knowing that there were two cities called Jericho in Jesus' day solves the apparent contradiction. Luke referred to the city that Jesus was approaching. Mark referred to the one that Jesus had left. The healing of the blind man occurred as Jesus traveled between the two. It is not the gospel writers who erred, but the critics of the Bible who are unfamiliar with first-century geography of the Holy Land.[25]

On the Gospels:

"All I am in private life is a literary critic and historian, that's my job...And I'm prepared to say on that basis if anyone thinks the Gospels are either legends or novels, then that person is simply showing his incompetence as a literary critic. I've read a great many novels and I know a fair amount about the legends that grew up among early people, and I know perfectly well the Gospels are not that kind of stuff."

C.S. Lewis (1898–1963), professor and author. *Christian Reflections* (Eerdmans, 1967), p. 209.

15. "Wasn't the New Testament written down hundreds of years after Jesus lived? Wouldn't that make it unreliable?"

There is actually good evidence that most of the New Testament was completed before AD 70.[26] For example, the New Testament Scriptures are absolutely silent regarding the destruction of the Jewish temple by the Romans in AD 70. This was one of the most significant events in all of Jewish history, and Jesus prophesied it would happen (Mark 13:1-2). The silence of the New Testament authors implies that their writings were completed prior to this event.

Second, the New Testament authors mentioned the names of rulers like Herod, Caiaphas, and Pontius Pilate, but they are completely silent regarding Caesar Nero and the incredible persecution he unleashed on the church in AD 64.

Third, the martyrdoms of Paul (AD 64) and Peter (AD 65) are not mentioned anywhere in the New Testament. The apostle

Paul was still alive at the end of Luke's second writing, the book of Acts (see Acts 28). This implies that Luke must have written his Gospel sometime prior.

Fourth, the pool of Bethesda, which was destroyed in AD 70, was still in existence when John wrote his Gospel (John 5:2). I could go on, but it is safe to say that the New Testament was completed before the close of the first century, within the lifetimes of the eyewitnesses and contemporaries of the events.[27]

On the Bible:

"Holy Scripture could never lie or err...its decrees are of absolute and inviolable truth."

Galileo Galilei (1564–1642), Italian physicist, astronomer, and philosopher, in a letter to Benedetto Castelli in 1613.

"Men do not reject the Bible because it contradicts itself, but because it contradicts them."

E. Paul Hovey

16. "Doesn't the Bible have scientific errors in it?"

The Bible may appear out of harmony with some modern-day theories, like the theory of Darwinian evolution, but when it comes to verifiable, provable scientific facts, the Bible agrees perfectly with the way things really are. The authors of the Bible not only spoke accurately about the universe in which we live but also revealed numerous facts about the universe thousands of years before modern scientists actually discovered them. I will give you three quick examples.

The first example has to do with the earth's shape. About 2600 years ago, when most of the world thought the earth was flat, Isaiah declared that the earth was actually a round sphere (Isaiah 40:22).

A second example has to do with the earth's suspension. In one of the oldest books in the Bible, Job proclaimed more than

4000 years ago that the earth hangs on nothing (Job 26:7). Not until 1650 did scientists discover that to be true. Hindus believed that the earth rested on the back of an elephant that stood on the back of a turtle that was swimming in a great endless sea.

A third example has to do with the sun. The Qur'an, written in the seventh century AD, says that the sun sets in a muddy spring (Surah 18:86). But David, writing about 1700 years before Muhammad, said the sun is actually on a circuit "from one end of heaven...to the other end" (Psalm 19:6).

How did Isaiah, Job, and David know these things? Second Peter 1:21 tells us that "holy men of God spoke as they were moved by the Holy Spirit." God, who knows all there is to know about the universe and the earth that He created, supernaturally superintended the authors of the Bible to make sure that what He wanted written was actually written.

On the Bible:

"There are more sure marks of authenticity in the Bible than in any profane history."

Sir Isaac Newton (1642–1727), physicist, mathematician, astronomer, inventor, philosopher, and alchemist. Quoted in *America's God and Country: Encyclopedia of Quotations* (Fame, 1994, p. 473).

17.

"How do you know that Christianity is true and not some other religion, like Buddhism or Islam?"

Jesus said it was. Jesus testified that the Bible, upon which Christianity is based, was without error (John 17:17), historically reliable (cf. Matthew 12:40; 24:37-39), divinely authoritative (Matthew 4:4-10), scientifically accurate regarding the origin of man (Matthew 19:4-5), infallible (John 10:35), and indestructible (Matthew 5:18). If Jesus was a prophet of God, as even the Qur'an teaches, or even if He was a good teacher, as so many are willing to believe, we would be wise to take His word on the matter.[28] Jesus proved that He was the trustworthy Son of God by His miraculous fulfillment of hundreds of Old Testament prophecies, His sinless life, His miracles, and His resurrection from the dead.[29] Buddha and Muhammad both admitted their sinfulness and performed no miracles, and both of their bodies are in their tombs to this day.[30] Jesus' grave is empty.[31] He is the reliable authority on life after death and spiritual matters.

On the Resurrection:

"I have been used for many years to study the histories of other times, and to examine and weigh the evidence of those who have written about them, and I know of no one fact in the history of mankind which is proved by better and fuller evidence of every sort, to the understanding of a fair inquirer, than the great sign which God hath given us that Christ died and rose again from the dead."

Thomas Arnold (1795–1842), professor and author. Cited in Josh McDowell, *Evidence That Demands a Verdict,* vol. 1 (Nelson, 1979), p. 191.

"The evidence for the resurrection is better than for claimed miracles in any other religion. It's outstandingly different in quality and quantity."

Antony Flew (1923–), British philosopher and author, in an interview with Gary Habermas. See www.biola.edu/antonyflew.

18. "What about homosexuals? Do you believe they go to hell?"

The Bible says that people who refuse to turn from their sin and receive God's forgiveness will end up in hell whether they be heterosexual or homosexual. Does the Bible teach that homosexuality is a sin? Yes, very clearly (see Leviticus 18:22; Romans 1:26-28; 1 Corinthians 6:9-10). But it also says that fornication (sex between an unmarried man and woman), lying, stealing, and drunkenness are sins. So let us lay aside the whole issue of homosexuality for a moment and imagine that our homosexual friends are married, monogamous heterosexuals. They still have a problem. They, like all of us, have broken a number of God's other commandments (Psalm 143:2). Regardless of the nature of their sin, all people, heterosexual or homosexual, must turn to the Lord and trust in Christ in order to be saved (Acts 4:12; 17:30-31).[32]

On Speaking with Skeptics:

"I confess that when I have to argue about the truth of divine things it is a dreary task to me…while they are wanting me to argue about this point or that it seems to me like asking a man to prove that there is a sun in yonder sky. I bask in His beams, I swoon under His heat, I see by His light; and yet they ask me to prove His existence! Are the men mad? What do they want me to prove? That God hears prayer? I pray and receive answers every day. That God pardons sin? I was in my own esteem the blackest of sinners, and sunk in the depths of despair, yet I believed, and by that faith I leaped into a fullness of light and liberty at once. Why do they not try it themselves?"

Charles H. Spurgeon (1834–1892), British preacher and author.

19. "How can you be sure Jesus rose from the dead?"

Here are a few quick reasons we can be sure. First, Christianity turned the world upside down 2000 years ago, beginning in the very city where the people demanded Jesus' crucifixion and where Jesus was publicly crucified and buried. The best explanation for the sudden birth of Christianity and its phenomenal growth is that Jesus really did rise from the dead.

Second, the early Christians were willing to suffer agonizing martyrdoms in order to testify that Jesus was alive.[33] The best explanation for their boldness and willingness to die was that they really did see Jesus alive after His crucifixion (1 Corinthians 15:3-7). Nobody willingly and knowingly dies for a lie.

Third, the Old Testament prophesied that the Messiah would rise from the dead (Psalm 16:10), and the New Testament says that Jesus did rise from the dead (Matthew 28:6). Hundreds of fulfilled prophecies, thousands of archaeological discoveries, and dozens of external sources (such as Flavius Josephus) have established the fact that the Bible is, at bare minimum, a historically reliable book.

Fourth, I would tell you about my own personal experience. Years ago I cried out to Jesus and said, "If You are alive, come into my life, forgive me of my sins, and be the Lord of my life." Many things since then have convinced me, beyond the shadow of a doubt, that He heard that prayer and is indeed alive and at work in my life.

On the Resurrection:

"Why would the apostles lie?...Liars always lie for selfish reasons. If they lied, what was their motive, what did they get out of it? What they got out of it was misunderstanding, rejection, persecution, torture, and martyrdom. Hardly a list of perks!"

Peter Kreeft, professor of philosophy. Norman L. Geisler and Paul K. Hoffman, eds., *Why I Am a Christian: Leading Thinkers Explain Why They Believe* (Baker, 2001), p. 232.

20. "What about evolution? Haven't Darwin's theories disproved God's existence?"

Darwin's theory of evolution does not in any way disprove the existence of God. The theory of evolution seeks only to explain how existing life forms have changed over time. Nobody disagrees that life forms have the ability to adapt to their environment. I believe this ability to adapt to the environment is actually evidence of design. And I am in good company. Hundreds of scientists from leading universities acknowledge that life is far too complex to have come about by some mindless process and random series of accidents.[34]

And evolutionists would be the first to admit that Darwin's theories do nothing to explain how life originated, or for that matter, how the entire universe came to be. If you hold to Darwin's theory of evolution, do not allow that to keep you back from acknowledging that there is a God who created the world and that you are a sinner in need of His grace and forgiveness. By believing that God exists, you'd be following in the footsteps of Antony Flew, who was widely considered the world's most influential atheistic philosopher, author, and debater. In 2004 Flew abandoned his atheism and acknowledged that God must exist. He said, "It now seems to me that the findings of more than fifty years of DNA research have provided materials for a new and enormously powerful argument to design." "What I think the DNA material has done is show that intelligence must have been involved."[35] What changed his mind? The complexity of the DNA inside living cells. Scientists are discovering that living cells could never have come into being apart from an intelligent designer. They are that complex.[36]

On Evolution:

"To suppose that the eye, with all its inimitable contrivances for adjusting the focus to different distances, for admitting different amounts of light, and for the correction of spherical and chromatic aberration, could have been formed by natural selection, seems, I freely confess, absurd in the highest possible degree."

Charles Darwin (1809–1882), British naturalist. *On the Origin of Species*, 1859, chapter 6. Available online at www.literature.org.

21. "If everything needs a maker, as Christians seem to suggest, who made God?"

Nobody. Everything that begins to exist requires a cause, but the Bible says that God is eternal, or without beginning (Psalm 90:2). That being the case, He did not need a maker or a cause. He is the Uncaused Cause, the Creator of all things (Isaiah 44:24; John 1:3).

On Evidence for a Designer:

"[Reason tells me of the] extreme difficulty or rather impossibility of conceiving this immense and wonderful universe, including man with his capability of looking far backwards and far into futurity, as the result of blind chance or necessity. When thus reflecting I feel compelled to look to a First Cause having an intelligent mind in some degree analogous to that of man; and I deserve to be called a Theist."

Charles Darwin, quoted in Antony Flew, *There Is a God: How the World's Most Notorious Atheist Changed His Mind* (HarperOne, 2007), p. 106.

"There is for me powerful evidence that there is something going on behind it all…It seems as though somebody has fine tuned nature's numbers to make the Universe…The impression of design is overwhelming."

Paul Davies (1946–), physicist and author. *The Cosmic Blueprint* (Simon & Schuster, 1988), p. 203.

On Evolution:

"Scientists who utterly reject evolution may be one of our fastest-growing controversial minorities…Many of the scientists supporting this position hold impressive credentials in science."

Larry Hatfield, "Educators Against Darwin," *Science Digest*, Winter 1979, pp. 94-96.

22. "If God doesn't need a maker, why couldn't we just say the universe doesn't need a maker either?"

God does not need a maker because He has always been. The universe has not always been. An overwhelming amount of evidence (including the motion of the galaxies, the second law of thermodynamics, and the background radiation echo) proves that the universe had a beginning. This fact is hardly debated within the scientific community. Logically, we know that anything that begins to exist must have a cause or a maker. Even David Hume, one of history's most zealous skeptics of Christianity, agreed to this fact when he said, "I never asserted so absurd a proposition as that anything might arise without a cause."[37] If the universe began to exist, and we know that it did, it must have a cause or maker. "Nothing" cannot, and does not, produce something.[38]

On the Universe:

"I myself find it hard to accept the notion of self-creation from nothing, even given unrestricted chance."

J.L. Mackie (1917–1981), philosopher and author. *Times Literary Supplement*, February 5, 1982, p. 126.

On Difficulties in Believing:

"I have noticed that whenever a person gives up his belief in the Word of God because it requires that he should believe a good deal, his unbelief requires him to believe a great deal more. If there be any difficulties in the faith of Christ, they are not one-tenth as great as the absurdities in any system of unbelief which seeks to take its place."

Charles H. Spurgeon (1834–1892), British preacher and author.

23. "Can God make a rock so big He cannot move it? Yes or No?"

A simple yes-or-no answer will not suffice for the question when it's worded this way. Either answer would suggest that God is not omnipotent (all-powerful), but the Bible clearly affirms that He is (Genesis 18:14; Luke 1:37). Your question is like asking someone, "Have you stopped beating your wife yet? Yes or No?" For the person who has not been beating his wife, a simple yes-or-no answer will not do. If he says yes, he implies that he used to beat his wife. If he says no, he implies that he is still beating his wife. The same is true with this question. A yes-or-no answer will not work.

God is omnipotent, so He can create any kind of rock He wants to, and He can lift any rock that He creates.[39]

On Apparent Design:

"A commonsense interpretation of the facts suggests that a superintellect has monkeyed with physics, as well as with chemistry and biology, and that there are no blind forces worth speaking about in nature. The numbers one calculates from the facts seem to me so overwhelming as to put this conclusion almost beyond question."

Fred Hoyle (1915–2001), British astronomer and professor. *The Universe: Some Past and Present Reflections* (Dept. of Applied Mathematics and Astronomy, University College, 1982) 20:16.

On the Fossil Record:

"The extreme rarity of transitional forms in the fossil record persists as the trade secret of paleontology. The evolutionary trees that adorn our textbooks have data only at the tips and nodes of their branches; the rest is inference, however reasonable, not the evidence of fossils."

Stephen Jay Gould (1941–2002), paleontologist, author, and professor. *The Panda's Thumb* (Norton, 1982), p. 181.

24. "How (or where) did Cain get his wife?"

∞

Obviously, he married someone in Adam and Eve's lineage—perhaps a sister or a niece.[40] The three boys mentioned in Genesis 4 (Cain, Abel and Seth) were not the only children Adam and Eve had. The very next chapter says that Adam and Eve had "other sons and daughters" (Genesis 5:4 NASB).

Some critics say, "Aha, but didn't God forbid incest?" No, not at that time. Only later, during the days of Moses (c. 1446 BC), after the gene pool had undergone years of contamination by sin, did the Lord forbid incest (see Leviticus 18–20).[41]

On Errors in Interpreting the Bible:

"In my experience when critics raise these objections, they invariably violate one of seventeen principles for interpreting the Scriptures…For example, assuming the unexplained is unexplainable…failing to understand the context of the passage…assuming a partial report is a false report…neglecting to interpret difficult passages in light of clear ones; basing a teaching on an obscure passage; forgetting that the Bible uses nontechnical, everyday language; failing to remember the Bible uses different literary devices…"

Norman Geisler (1932–), from his interview in Lee Strobel, *The Case for Faith* (Zondervan, 2000), pp. 137–38.

On Archaeology:

"It may be stated categorically that no archaeological discovery has ever controverted a biblical reference. Scores of archeological findings have been made which confirm in clear outline or exact detail historical statements in the Bible. And, by the same token, proper evaluation of biblical descriptions has often led to amazing discoveries."

Nelson Glueck (1900–1971), archaeologist and author. *Rivers in the Desert* (Farrar, Straus and Cudahy, 1959), p. 136.

25.
"How can you adhere to a religion that would advocate such events as the Crusades?"

The Crusades were carried out nearly a thousand years ago in the name of Christianity, but the violence that occurred contradicted the teachings of Christ. Jesus told His disciples to love their enemies (Matthew 5:44). As Jesus was being arrested on the eve of His crucifixion, Peter pulled out his sword and struck the ear of Malchus, the servant of the high priest. Jesus healed the man's ear and told Peter to put away his sword (Luke 22:50-51; John 18:11). Even as Jesus was dying on the cross, He asked His Father to forgive His murderers (Luke 23:34). God's kingdom was never to be advanced with violence. Do not let the unchristian behavior of men a thousand years ago keep you from receiving God's gift of eternal life! (See Romans 6:23.)

On Jesus:

"Alexander, Caesar, Charlemagne, and myself founded empires; but upon what foundation did we rest the creations of our genius? Upon force! But Jesus Christ founded His upon love; and at this hour millions of men would die for Him."

Napoleon Bonaparte I (1769–1821), emperor of France. Quoted in *America's God and Country: Encyclopedia of Quotations* (Fame, 1994), p. 463.

On the Bible:

"We are fortunate to have the Bible and especially the New Testament, which tells us so much about God in widely accessible human terms."

Arthur Schawlow (1921–1999), professor and Nobel Prize winner.

26. "What about the Old Testament, where Joshua and the nation of Israel were commanded by God to go through the land of Canaan and destroy everyone? How can you believe in a God who would command such a thing?"

We need to remember at least three things when we consider the story of Joshua.

First, God is sovereign over His creation. He created us, and He has the right to do with us as He deems best. If you plant a garden in your backyard, you have the right to do with it as you see fit. You can pluck those plants up whenever you want. Your neighbor does not have that right because those plants do not belong to him. The same is true with God. People belong to God, and He can end a life (or lives) whenever and however He thinks best.

Second, the people of Canaan were guilty of terrible sins. They were burning their children as sacrifices to the god Molech. They were having sexual relations with animals (Leviticus 18:21-24). They hated the Hebrew people and would have destroyed them. This would have prohibited the Messiah, the future Savior for all mankind, from being born into the world, for God promised that He would be a descendant of Abraham.

Third, keep in mind that God patiently allowed the people of Canaan more than 400 years to repent (Genesis 15:16-21). Had they repented like the people of Nineveh did (Jonah 3), God would have spared them (Jeremiah 18:7-8).

27. "Do you think it's right to try to force your beliefs on other people?"

No. Nowhere in the Gospels do we see Jesus coercing people to believe. The New Testament tells us that "He went through every city and village, preaching and bringing the glad tidings of the kingdom of God" (Luke 8:1). He simply shared the good news, and that is what He sent out His disciples to do (Luke 9:2). Jesus does not kick doors down and force Himself into a person's life (Revelation 3:20). He waits to be received (John 1:12). He allows people to freely choose (Matthew 22:3; John 5:39-40) whom they will follow (Matthew 23:37; Joshua 24:15).

So is it right to try to force our beliefs on other people? No. Is it right to humbly, gently, and respectfully share the good news about all that God has done?[42] Absolutely. After that, it is up to them to decide whether to believe.

On Truth:

"Truth is so obscured nowadays and lies [are] so well established that unless we love the truth we shall never recognize it."

Blaise Pascal (1623–1662), mathematician, scientist, philosopher. Quoted in Peter Kreeft, *Christianity for Modern Pagans: Pascal's Pensées* (Ignatius Press, 1993), p. 216.

"If you abide in My word, you are My disciples indeed. And you shall know the truth, and the truth shall make you free."

John 8:31-32

On Atheist's Conversion:

"I heard the story of a man, a blasphemer…an atheist, who was converted singularly by a sinful action of his. He had written on a piece of paper, 'God is nowhere,' and ordered his child to read it, for he would make him an atheist too. The child spelled it, "God is n-o-w h-e-r-e. God is now here." It was a truth instead of a lie, and the arrow pierced the man's own heart."

Charles H. Spurgeon (1834–1892), British preacher and author.

28.

"Isn't there evidence that the New Testament authors borrowed their idea for Jesus' resurrection from ancient pagan religions that were around long before the time of Christ?"

No. That is a rumor that has gained some momentum as of late, but there is not one clear case of any alleged resurrection that appears in any pagan text before the late second century AD, almost 100 years after the New Testament was written. If there was any influence of one religion on the other, it was the influence of Christianity on mythology. It is likely that the pagan religions, observing the growth of Christianity, began to mimic its beliefs.

The only known account of a god surviving death that predates Christianity is the Egyptian cult god Osiris. In this myth, Osiris is cut into 14 pieces, scattered around Egypt, and then reassembled and brought back to life by the goddess Isis. However,

Osiris does not actually come back to physical life but becomes a member of a shadowy underworld. This is far different from Jesus' resurrection. And even if myths about gods dying and rising did exist prior to Christianity, that doesn't mean the New Testament writers copied from them. The fictional TV show *Star Trek* preceded the U.S. Space Shuttle program, but we never saw newspaper reports of space shuttle missions being influenced by *Star Trek* episodes![43]

On Alleged Parallels:

"Many Christian college students have encountered criticisms of Christianity based on claims that early Christianity and the New Testament borrowed important beliefs and practices from a number of pagan mystery religions...the evidence for such claims, when it even exists, often lies in sources several centuries [after] the New Testament. Moreover, the alleged parallels often result from liberal scholars uncritically describing pagan beliefs and practices in Christian language and then marveling at the striking parallels they think they've discovered."

Ronald Nash, "Was the New Testament Influenced by Pagan Religions?" Available at AlwaysBeReady.com.

29. "Why aren't dinosaurs mentioned in the Bible?"

First, we should not expect to see the word *dinosaur* in the Bible. The term was not coined until a famous paleontologist, Sir Richard Owen, gave them that name in 1841—nearly 18 centuries after the New Testament was finished.[44]

Second, just because a creature is not mentioned in the Bible does not mean that it did not exist. Thousands of creatures are not specifically mentioned in the Bible, including giraffes, alligators, and penguins.

Third, the Bible does actually mention at least two different creatures that very well may have been dinosaurs: behemoth and leviathan. Behemoth is described as having a tail like a cedar tree (Job 40:15-19). Of Leviathan, the Lord said to Job, "Indeed, any hope of overcoming him is false; shall one not be overwhelmed at the sight of him? No one is so fierce that he would dare stir him up…Who can remove his outer coat? Who can approach him with a double bridle? Who can open the doors of his face, with his terrible teeth all around? His rows of scales are his pride" (Job 41:9-10,13-15). Scales? Terrible teeth? So fierce that no one would dare wake him up? It is easy to see why numerous biblical scholars have concluded that Leviathan may have been a dinosaur.

On Intelligent Design:

"When you analyze all of the most current affirmative evidence from cosmology, physics, astronomy, biology, and so forth…the positive case for an intelligent designer becomes absolutely compelling."

Jonathan Wells, scientist, in Lee Strobel, *The Case for a Creator* (Zondervan, 2004), p. 66.

"The most beautiful system of the sun, planets and comets could only proceed from the counsel and dominion of an intelligent and powerful being."

Sir Isaac Newton (1642–1727), physicist, mathematician, astronomer, inventor, philosopher, and alchemist. Cited in *Newton's Philosophy of Nature: Selections from His Writings* (Hafner, 1953), p. 42.

30. "How could dinosaurs fit on Noah's ark? If dinosaurs were on Noah's ark, why aren't they around today?"

Those are great questions. First, bear in mind that the ark described in the Bible was not the 45- to 50-foot model made popular in children's books. It was extremely large. According to the measurements given in the Bible (Genesis 6:15), it was about 450 feet long, 75 feet wide, and 45 feet tall (4.5 stories)!

Second, remember that not all dinosaurs were large, like the brachiosaur. Many of them, like the compsognathus, were quite small, even just a few pounds. Even the biggest dinosaurs came from eggs no larger than footballs.[45]

Third, Noah probably took young dinosaurs with him, rather than the older and larger ones. The smaller ones would have been easier to fit in the ark, feed, and take care of, and they would have been in better shape than older ones for repopulating the earth.

Fourth, remember that Noah was not required to bring two of every type of dinosaur on the ark, but only two of every kind (Genesis 6:20), a much smaller number.[46] Fitting the dinosaurs on the ark would have been no problem.[47]

As for why we do not see dinosaurs around today, keep in mind that the flood occurred approximately 2300 or 2400 years before Christ, more than 4000 years ago. As for those dinosaurs that survived the flood aboard Noah's ark, we are not sure why their offspring did not continue indefinitely. They may have died off for some of the same reasons other creatures have become extinct. Perhaps they were overhunted. Perhaps an ice age or severe change in the environment that came after the flood affected the lush vegetation that many of them depended on for food. Only God knows for sure. The existence of billions of dead animals, including dinosaurs, encased in sedimentary rock (which, interestingly, is rock that has been laid down by water) averaging a mile deep on all seven continents, is an amazing evidence that the flood actually did occur (Genesis 6:17; 7:4).[48]

31. "How could all the races, with their different skin colors, come from Noah's family?"

We need to keep two facts in mind when we consider this question.[49] First, there is only one race—the human race. The Chinese, Africans, Eskimos, Indians, and Australian Aborigines are all *Homo sapiens*. When it comes to the basic structure of the human body, all of these groups have the same amount of bones and the same organs, and they can all successfully interbreed with one another. The primary difference between these different groups is their skin color.

Second, keep in mind that there is really only one skin color: melanin. Melanin is the brownish pigment that we all have in our skin and that protects the skin from the sun's damaging ultraviolet light. If people's bodies produce only a little melanin, they will have fairer skin. If their bodies produce a lot of melanin, they will be dark brown. In between are all the lighter shades of brown. God created our bodies with an amazing ability to adapt to our environment. People groups who have lived in colder climates for a long time (such as northern Europe), where there is not much sunlight, have developed fairer skin. People groups who have lived nearer to the equator (like in Africa or South America), where the sun is more intense, have developed darker skin.

Why would God design humans with this built-in capability? It is important for our survival. If you have too little melanin in your skin (you are fair skinned) and live in a very sunny environment, you will easily burn and develop skin cancer. If you have a great deal of melanin (darker skin) and you live in a country where there is little sunshine (Finland, for example), you may struggle to get enough vitamin D, which needs sunshine for its production in your body. A vitamin D deficiency can cause bone disorders, such as rickets.

32. "Don't all religions basically teach the same thing?"

That is a popular belief, but the answer is no. The religions of the world are vastly different and even contradictory in many of their core teachings.

For example, consider some of the different views regarding the nature of God. Some religions, like Islam, Christianity, and Judaism, teach that God is the transcendent Creator of the world and that He is distinct and separate from His creation. Other religions, like Hinduism, teach that God and the physical universe are one and the same. Some religions teach that God is a he, some say a she, some say an it. Mormonism, Shinto, and different tribal religions teach that there are many gods. Adherents to the New Age movement and Christian Science believe that *we* are God.

Consider the different views of salvation and what that even means. Judaism, Islam, and Christianity teach that salvation means eternal life in heaven. To Buddhists, it means an indescribable, almost nonexistent state known as parinirvana. To the majority of Jehovah's Witnesses, it means everlasting life on earth. The goal of Hindus is to break free from the cycle of life, death, and reincarnation and have their individual personality annihilated by becoming absorbed into Brahman.

Consider how salvation is obtained. The Bible teaches that salvation is a gift given by a gracious God to all who receive it by faith. The Qur'an says you can obtain salvation if you submit yourself to Allah and His laws and your good works outweigh your bad works. Hinduism's ultimate goal is said to be obtained by achieving a certain state of consciousness in which people realize their identity with God. Buddhism's ultimate goal is said to be achievable to those who eliminate all desires—even the desire to live.

When it comes to the nature of God, salvation, and how that salvation is obtained, the world's religions contain many contradictory teachings.

33. "Don't Christians worship the same God as Muslims?"

No. There are some major differences between the god presented in the Qur'an and the God of the Bible. The Qur'an teaches that Allah is not triune (Father, Son, and Holy Spirit), but the God of the Bible is. To say that God has a Son, as the Bible does, is an unforgivable sin known as *shirk* to Muslims.[50]

God's love also sets Him apart from the god put forth in the Qur'an. The Qur'an states over and over again that Allah does not love ungrateful sinners, unbelievers, the proud, or the extravagant.[51] The God of the Bible loves the whole world, including sinners. Jesus said, "For God so loved the world [that would include everyone] that He gave His only begotten Son, that whoever believes in Him should not perish but have everlasting life" (John 3:16). The Bible says elsewhere that "God demonstrates His own love toward us, in that while we were still sinners,

Christ died for us" (Romans 5:8). That is good news for those of us who realize we are sinners.

The Bible also teaches that those who put their faith in Christ are adopted into God's family (Ephesians 1:5) and can personally address God as "Father" (Matthew 6:9; Romans 8:15). The God of the Bible offers mankind a personal relationship of great intimacy. That is not the case in Islam, which has no fatherly concept of God. To most Muslims, Allah is seen more as a remote judge who is not personally involved with mankind. Islam is not about fellowship with God, but service, submission, and allegiance to God.[52]

These are just some of the differences between the god put forth in the Qur'an and the God of the Bible. The god portrayed in the Qur'an is not the God spoken of in the Bible and, in fact, does not even exist (Isaiah 46:9).

On God:

"I, even I, am the LORD, and besides Me there is no savior...I am God, and there is no other; I am God, and there is none like Me."

Isaiah 43:11; 46:9

34. "What makes you think the Qur'an is not divinely inspired?"

There are numerous reasons for doubting that the Qur'an is inspired.[53] First, it contradicts authentic Scripture, the Bible. For instance, it teaches that God does not love sinners (see, for example, Surah 2:276) and that people obtain salvation when their good works outweigh their bad works (Surah 23:102-3). The Bible teaches that God loves sinners (Romans 5:8) and that salvation comes to us solely through God's grace (Ephesians 2:8-9).

Second, it contradicts known facts of science. For example, it teaches that the sun actually descends down into a muddy spring on the earth (Surah 18:86). You could get away with a statement like that in certain parts of the world in the seventh century. Obviously, today, we know that the sun is actually on a circuit through space.[54]

Third, the Qur'an contradicts known facts of history. For example, it denies that Jesus of Nazareth was crucified on a cross (Surah 4:157), something that has been substantiated not only by the Bible but also by extrabiblical sources, such as the Jewish Talmud and Flavius Josephus.

Fourth, the Qur'an is plagued with internal inconsistencies.[55]

Fifth, there are no particularly good reasons to accept the Qur'an as inspired Scripture. The most popular evidence that Muslims put forth for the divine inspiration of the Qur'an is its literary beauty, but this is a highly questionable means of testing a document for divine inspiration. What would stop us from believing that Shakespeare's writings were also divinely inspired? For these reasons, and others, it is safe to conclude that the Qur'an is not divinely inspired.

On the Crucifixion:

"As a Muslim I came to believe that the crucifixion of Christ was an undisputable historical fact that no honest person that deals with evidences of history could deny."

Abdul Saleeb, coauthor of *Answering Islam: The Crescent in the Light of the Cross* (Baker, 2002). See his testimony at www.leaderu.com /wri/pages/abdul.html.

35. "What makes you think the Book of Mormon is not trustworthy?"

The Book of Mormon is riddled with problems.

- It contradicts authentic Scripture (the Bible).[56]
- It contains false prophecy.[57]
- Many doctrinal and grammatical changes have been made since its initial publishing in 1830.[58]
- It contains extensive plagiarism of the King James Version of the Bible.[59]
- Independent, non-Mormon archaeological verification is absolutely lacking.[60]
- If that were not enough, the Book of Mormon is permeated with scientific problems.[61]

The open-minded individual who is willing to follow the

evidence (or in this case, lack of evidence) wherever it leads can easily see that the Book of Mormon is an early nineteenth-century piece of American fiction. Orson Pratt (1811–1881), one of the early leaders in the Mormon church, said, "The Book of Mormon claims to be a divinely inspired record…If false [he did not think it was], it is one of the most cunning, wicked, bold, deep-laid impositions ever palmed upon the world, calculated to deceive and ruin millions."[62] The Book of Mormon *can* be proven to be false, and therefore Pratt's words stand. I could not have said it better myself. *That* is what the Book of Mormon is.

On the Book of Mormon:

"Archaeologists and other scholars have long probed the hemisphere's past, and the Society does not know of anything found so far that has substantiated the Book of Mormon."

From a letter from the National Geographic Society dated August 12, 1998. View the entire letter at irr.org/mit/national-geographic.html.

"One of the most modern pretenders to inspiration is the Book of Mormon. I could not blame you should you laugh outright while I read aloud a page from that farrago."

Charles H. Spurgeon (1834–1892), British preacher and author.

36. "If Christianity is true, why can't different denominations agree on what to believe?"

Actually, Christian denominations agree on many important issues. When it comes to the core, foundational beliefs of Christianity, Christian churches are very unified. They do have different opinions on some issues (such as what kind of worship music is best and how a local church should be governed), but when it comes to the authenticity of the Bible, the deity of Christ, what His death on the cross accomplished, His bodily resurrection from the grave, and His second coming, there is great harmony.

It is important to realize that disagreements over the facts do not weaken or negate the facts. For centuries man debated and disagreed about the shape of the earth. Some said it was round. Some thought it was flat. During that time, the earth never ceased to be round. The same is true with Christianity.

The different denominations may disagree about certain aspects of church life or worship styles, but the facts stay the same. Jesus is both Lord and God, and He is worthy of our trust and worship.

On Jesus:

"This Jesus of Nazareth, without money and arms, conquered more millions than Alexander, Caesar, Mohammed, and Napoleon; without science and learning, He shed more light on things human and divine than all philosophers and scholars combined; without the eloquence of schools, He spoke such words of life as were never spoken before or since, and produced effects which lie beyond the reach of orator or poet; without writing a single line, He set more pens in motion, and furnished themes for more sermons, orations, discussions, learned volumes, works of art, and songs of praise than the whole army of great men of ancient and modern times."

Philip Schaff (1819–1893), historian. *The Person of Christ* (American Tract Society, 1913), pp. 29-30.

37. "Aren't there a bunch of hypocrites in the church?"

Perhaps there are. What better place for them to be? That is where they will be exposed to the Word of God and learn that hypocrisy is wrong (Matthew 23:28). Do not allow the sins of others to keep you from receiving God's gift of eternal life (Romans 6:23). God will deal with them. The Bible says, "Each of us shall give account of himself to God" (Romans 14:12).

On Evolution:

"One of the reasons I started taking this anti-evolutionary view, or let's call it non-evolutionary view, was last year I had a sudden realization that for over twenty years I had thought I was working on evolution in some way. One morning I woke up and something had happened in the night and it struck me that I had been working on this stuff for twenty years and there was not one thing I knew about it. That's quite a shock to learn that one can be misled so long…. For the last few weeks I've tried putting a simple question to various people and groups of people. The question is this: Can you tell me anything you know about evolution, any one thing, any one thing that you think is true? I tried that question on the geology staff at the Field Museum of Natural History and the only answer I got was silence. I tried it on the members of the Evolutionary Morphology Seminar at the University of Chicago, a very prestigious body of evolutionists, and all I got there was silence for a long time and eventually one person said, 'I do know one thing—it ought not to be taught in high school'…The level of knowledge about evolution is remarkably shallow. We know it ought not to be taught in the high school and that's all we know about it."

Colin Patterson, former senior paleontologist at the British Museum of Natural History and editor of its journal. Quoted in Norman Geisler and Peter Bocchino, *Unshakable Foundations* (Bethany, 2001), p. 167.

38. "Does it really matter what people believe as long as they are sincere?"

It certainly does matter. Regarding faith in Jesus, the Bible says that "there is salvation in no one else; for there is no other name under heaven that has been given among men by which we must be saved" (Acts 4:12 NASB). People cannot put their faith in the god of Mormonism, a god who (according to Joseph Smith) was once a mere man who became one of many gods, and hope that god will save them or forgive them of their sins. That god does not exist. That god was a nineteenth-century invention by Joseph Smith.

Millions of sincere Muslims around the world are putting their faith in Allah, the god set forth in the Qur'an, but how is Allah going to save them? The god described in the Qur'an does not exist.[63]

No amount of sincerity in the heart of a Mormon or Muslim

will raise either one of these gods into being. Sincere faith is only as useful as its object. A person can sincerely put his faith in a piece of yarn tied around his ankle as he bungee jumps off of the Empire State Building, but the yarn will not save him.

People who sincerely believe in Jesus, the true and living God who actually exists, are in good hands (John 10:27-30). Sincerity is important (Joshua 24:14; John 4:24), but God desires that we sincerely put our faith in *Him,* for He alone can save a person (Hosea 13:4). The gods of Hinduism, Mormonism, and Islam do not exist (Isaiah 43:10) and therefore cannot save even the sincerest of followers.

On Facts:

"If Christianity was something we were making up, of course we could make it easier. But it is not. We cannot compete, in simplicity, with people who are inventing religions. How could we? We are dealing with Fact. Of course anyone can be simple if he has no facts to bother about."

C.S. Lewis (1898–1963), professor and author. *Mere Christianity,* 1960, p. 145.

39. "How could I ever be happy in heaven, knowing that my loved ones are in hell?"

It is hard to imagine being happy without our loved ones. Maybe one of the reasons God has caused us to cross paths is so that you might receive of His grace and mercy and become the instrument He uses to reach your loved ones. He does not desire that any go to hell (Ezekiel 33:11). The Bible says that God is "not willing that any should perish but that all should come to repentance" (2 Peter 3:9). He is looking for someone whom He can use to help reach them (see also Isaiah 6:8; Ezekiel 22:30).

My friend, even if your loved ones reject everything you would tell them and end up in hell, God promises us that in His presence there is "fullness of joy" (Psalm 16:11). He also says that He is going to wipe away every tear from our eyes, and there shall no longer be any mourning, or crying, or pain (Revelation 21:4).

If you are concerned about your loved ones who may not go to heaven, the most irrational thing you could do is pass up God's offer of forgiveness and not go there yourself. Turn from your sins, put your faith in Christ, and allow Him to use you to reach out to them and others with the gospel.

On Coming to Jesus:

"When a person refuses to come to Christ it is never just because of lack of evidence or because of intellectual difficulties: at root, he refuses to come because he willingly ignores and rejects the drawing of God's Spirit on his heart. No one in the final analysis really fails to become a Christian because of lack of arguments; he fails to become a Christian because he loves darkness rather than light and wants nothing to do with God."

William Lane Craig, *Reasonable Faith: Christian Truth and Apologetics* (Crossway, 1994), p. 35.

40.

"Isn't being a good person enough to get to heaven?"

∞

That is certainly a popular belief today. From man's perspective, a person might appear to be a good person, but to God, who sees into the human heart, we are all unrighteous.[64] Jesus Himself said, "No one is good but One, that is, God" (Luke 18:19). Romans 3:10 says, "There is none righteous, no, not one." Isaiah 53:6 says, "All we like sheep have gone astray; we have turned, every one, to his own way." Obviously, some people are not as evil as they could be, and some are worse than others. The bottom line is this: We all need the grace and forgiveness God offers if we are to escape the judgment we deserve and go to heaven.

Two thousand years ago, God, out of His great love for you and me, came to earth as a man and died on a cruel Roman cross. There on the cross, He took upon Himself the punishment and judgment that was due sinners (Isaiah 53:5). He rose from the grave three days later and is now graciously offering forgiveness and everlasting life (John 3:16) to all who will acknowledge their sinfulness (1 John 1:8-10), turn from their sins (Acts 17:30), and put their faith in Jesus Christ as their Lord and Savior (Romans 10:9-10). If you do that, you will be saved (Acts 16:31). The Bible teaches that if you go on sinning willfully after receiving the knowledge of the truth, "there is only the terrible expectation of God's judgment and the raging fire that will consume his enemies" (Hebrews 10:27 NLT). The best decision you could ever make is to turn to Jesus, even right now, before it is too late.

On Salvation:

"We have believed in Christ Jesus, so that we might be made right with God by faith in Christ, not because we have obeyed the law. For no one will ever be made right with God by obeying the law...For if keeping the law could make us right with God, then there was no need for Christ to die."

Galatians 2:16,21 NLT

Steps to Peace with God

1. Acknowledge that you are a sinner.

    The Bible says that all of us have broken God's com-
    mandments. "There is none righteous, no, not one...all
    have sinned" (Romans 3:10,23). "If we say that we have
    no sin, we deceive ourselves" (1 John 1:8).

2. Believe that Jesus Christ died on the cross for you.

    The Bible says, "If you confess with your mouth Jesus
    as Lord, and believe in your heart that God raised Him
    from the dead, you will be saved" (Romans 10:9 NASB).
    Jesus said, "For God so loved the world that He gave His
    only begotten Son, that whoever believes in Him should
    not perish but have everlasting life" (John 3:16).

3. Change direction. Turn away from your sinful way of life.

    The Bible says, "God is now declaring to men that all
    people everywhere should repent [*repent* means to change
    direction, that is, turn away from your sins], because
    He has fixed a day in which He will judge the world in

righteousness" (Acts 17:30-31 NASB). If you are willing to repent, God will begin to change you and help you live a life that is pleasing to Him.

You can have your sins forgiven right now and begin experiencing a relationship with God today. Pray something like this:

God, I confess that I am a sinner. I realize that I need Your forgiveness. I believe that You, Jesus, paid the price for my sins on the cross. I believe that You rose again from the dead and want to have a relationship with me. Thank You. Come into my life. Forgive me. Be my Lord. Be my God. I want to turn away from my sins and begin to follow You. Change me. Empower me with Your Holy Spirit to live my life for You. Amen.

If you prayed that prayer with a sincere heart, you have begun a relationship with Jesus Christ, and God has forgiven you of your sins.

I encourage you to...

1. Begin reading and obeying the Bible. Try starting out with the Gospel of Luke in the New Testament, and follow that up by reading the book of Acts.

2. Begin praying. Simply talk to God. He loves you and wants to have a relationship with you.

3. Begin going to a church that teaches through the Bible and where the people love to worship the Lord. If they have a new believer's class, sign up to attend.

4. Make friends with other believers who can encourage you and be a blessing to you in your new relationship with Jesus. If you have friends or family members who are Christians, call them and let them know of the decision you have made.

Notes

Dedication. In 2002, the Southern Baptist Council on Family Life reported that 88 percent of children raised in evangelical homes leave church at the age of 18, never to return. Cited at www.pastors.com/RWMT/?ID=73. Accessed on October 15, 2005.

1. I have found this question (Do you have any spiritual beliefs?) to be much better than asking, "Do you believe in God?" William Fay discusses this in his excellent and helpful book on evangelism, *Share Jesus Without Fear* (Broadman & Holman, 1999).

2. For more on the evidence for God's existence, go to the link "Existence of God" at AlwaysBeReady.com.

3. For example, consider some of the Old Testament prophecies made regarding the Messiah, whom the Old Testament prophets said would come. They prophesied hundreds of years in advance that...

    He would be born of the seed of Abraham (Genesis 12:1-3; 22:18), of the tribe of Judah (Genesis 49:10),

of the house of David (2 Samuel 7:12-13),

in the city of Bethlehem (Micah 5:2),

to a virgin (Isaiah 7:14).

He would come while the temple was still standing (Malachi 3:1)

and perform miracles (Isaiah 35:5-6),

be rejected by His own people (Psalm 118:22; compare 1 Peter 2:7),

and die at a precise time in history (Daniel 9:24-26)

and in a certain manner (Psalm 22:16-18; Isaiah 53; Zechariah 12:10)

and rise from the dead (Psalm 16:10; compare with Acts 2:27-32).

All of these prophecies and hundreds of others have been fulfilled literally. For additional examples of fulfilled prophecies in the Bible, see *Every Prophecy of the Bible* by John Walvoord (Cook Communications, 2004).

4. Some verses in the Bible do appear on the surface to contradict each other, but with a little investigation into the original languages, the cultural context, and the geographical settings, these apparent disagreements are easily reconciled. See my study entitled, "An Examination of Apparent Contradictions in the Bible" at AlwaysBeReady.com, where I discuss the solutions to popularly cited apparent contradictions in the Bible. To find this study, click on the link "Bible."

5. For more on the trustworthiness of the Bible, go to the link "Bible" at AlwaysBeReady.com.

6. Norman L. Geisler, *Baker Encyclopedia of Christian Apologetics* (Baker, 1999), p. 187.

7. Examples include Tertullian, Justin Martyr, Eusebius, and Polycarp.

8. An excellent book that addresses the Bible's manuscript evidence is Norman Geisler and William Nix, *A General Introduction to the Bible*, revised and expanded edition (Moody, 1986). I have also written a brief article on this topic. Go to the link "Bible, Evidence for" at AlwaysBeReady.com.

9. For more help answering objections to the Bible's teaching on hell, go to the link "Hell" at AlwaysBeReady.com.

10. Lee Strobel, *The Case for Christ* (Zondervan, 1998), p. 260.

11. Flavius Josephus, *The Antiquities of the Jews,* 18:63-64 (Hendrickson, 1987), p. 480.

12. The Babylonian Talmud: Tractate Sanhedrin, Folio 43a, 33-34. See also John 19:14; Luke 22:15.

13. An excellent book on the evidence for Jesus' life is Gary Habermas, *The Historical Jesus: Ancient Evidence for the Life of Christ* (College Press, 1996).

A FOXNews.com headline (November 8, 2005) read, "Israel Church a Major Discovery." Here is an excerpt from that report:

Israeli prisoner Ramil Razilo was removing rubble from the planned site of a new prison ward when his shovel uncovered the edge of an elaborate mosaic, unveiling what Israeli archaeologists said Sunday may be the Holy Land's oldest church. The discovery of the church in the northern Israeli town of Megiddo, near the biblical Armageddon, was hailed by experts as an important discovery that could reveal details about the development of the early church in the region. Archaeologists said the church dated from the third century, decades before Constantine legalized Christianity across the Roman Empire...Channel Two television, which first reported the story, broadcast pictures of a detailed and well-preserved mosaic bearing the name of Jesus Christ in ancient Greek and images of fish.

CNN.com gave this report:

Two mosaics inside the church—one covered with fish, an ancient Christian symbol that predates the cross— tell the story of a Roman officer and a woman named Aketous who donated money to build the church in the memory "of the god, Jesus Christ."

This discovery not only affirms that Jesus lived but also helps to verify that the early church believed He was God.

14. Jesus said, "I am the way, the truth, and the life. No one comes to the Father except through Me" (John 14:6). Regarding faith in Jesus, Peter said, "There is salvation in no one else; for there is no other name under heaven that has been given

among men by which we must be saved" (Acts 4:12 NASB). Also see Matthew 7:13-14; 1 Timothy 2:5; Isaiah 43:11.

15. An examination of some of the Ten Commandments is all that is necessary to realize that Romans 3:10 is true when it states, "There is none righteous, no, not one." In Exodus 20, God states, "You shall have no other gods before Me...You shall not take the name of the LORD your God in vain, for the LORD will not hold him guiltless who takes His name in vain...Honor your father and your mother...You shall not murder. You shall not commit adultery. You shall not steal. You shall not bear false witness against your neighbor. You shall not covet your neighbor's house; you shall not covet your neighbor's wife...nor anything that is your neighbor's."

16. This is something that Dan Brown purports in his popular yet highly inaccurate novel *The Da Vinci Code* (Doubleday, 2003), p. 233. For a response to many of the book's erroneous claims, go to the link "Da Vinci Code" at AlwaysBeReady.com.

17. For more help defending the Bible's teaching regarding the deity of Christ, go to the link "Deity of Christ" at Always BeReady.com.

18. Ignatius (AD 30–98 or 107), the Bishop of Antioch, referred to Jesus as "Jesus Christ our God," "Jesus...who is God and man," "My God," "Our God Jesus Christ," and "God Incarnate." He wrote that "there is One God who manifests himself through Jesus Christ his son." Dr. Erwin Lutzer points out that the fact that Ignatius was not rebuked or branded as a heretic by any churches or Christian leaders

proves that the early church, long before the Council of Nicea in AD 325, believed that Jesus was God. Justin Martyr (AD 100–165) said Jesus, "being the first-begotten Word of God, is even God," and described Him as "both God and Lord of hosts." Irenaeus (AD 120–202) called Jesus "our Lord, and God, and Savior, and King." Clement of Alexandria (AD 150–215) said Jesus was "truly most manifest Deity, He that is made equal to the Lord of the universe; because He was His Son."

19. C.S. Lewis, *The Problem of Pain*. Cited in Wayne Martindale and Jerry Root, eds., *The Quotable Lewis* (Tyndale, 1989).

20. This last sentence is a paraphrase of J.P. Moreland's comments in Lee Strobel's interview of him in *The Case for Faith* (Zondervan, 2000), p. 178.

21. For example, consider these demeaning words that the Gospel of Thomas puts in the mouths of the apostle Peter and Jesus in verse 114. Peter supposedly says, "Make Mary leave us, for females don't deserve life." Jesus said, "Look, I will guide her to make her male, so that she too may become a living spirit resembling you males. For every female who makes herself male will enter the domain of heaven." Sayings like these made it obvious to the early Christians that these Gnostic gospels were not authentic, divinely inspired Scripture.

22. By *Apocrypha* I am referring to 14 Jewish writings, written between 200 BC and AD 100, after the completion of the Old Testament and before the establishment of the New Testament. Today, 11 of those books (including Tobit, Judith, First and Second Maccabees, and Baruch) are accepted by

the Catholic Church as God-inspired Scripture and are even placed in the Catholic Bible. For more information on the Apocrypha, go to the link "Catholicism" at AlwaysBeReady .com.

23. For example, Judith 1:1 tell us that Nebuchadnezzar reigned in the city of Nineveh. This was never the case. Nebuchadnezzar was the king of Babylonia in Babylon. Elsewhere in the Apocrypha, we are told that Tobit was alive when the Assyrians conquered Israel in 722 BC and also when Jeroboam revolted against Judah in 931 BC, which would make him at least 209 years old. Yet according to Tobit 14:11, he died at 158.

24. The New Testament book of Jude (9, 14-15) includes some allusions to extrabiblical writings, such as the Book of Enoch and the Bodily Assumption of Moses. Keep in mind that Jude does not cite these books as being inspired Scripture or divinely authoritative. He simply refers to a truth contained in those books which otherwise may have many errors. I mention this to make clear that these citations do not lend any support to the Catholic position, for even the Roman Catholic Church rejects those two particular books as noncanonical.

25. I would recommend that every student of the Bible own Norman Geisler and Thomas Howe's *The Big Book of Bible Difficulties* (Baker Books, 2008). It is an excellent handbook on Bible difficulties. Make sure to read the introduction, where the authors examine 17 mistakes critics make when interpreting the Bible. Two other excellent resources are

Gleason Archer, *New International Encyclopedia of Bible Difficulties* (Zondervan, 2001) and Walter Kaiser, Peter Davids, F.F. Bruce, and Manfred Brauch, *Hard Sayings of the Bible* (IVP, 1996). Also, many apologetics websites address apparent Bible contradictions. For instance, see carm.org and christiananswers.net.

26. Even John A.T. Robinson, a liberal scholar, concedes in his book *Redating the New Testament* (Westminster Press, 1976) that past scholarship suggesting a late completion date for the New Testament was based on a "tyranny of unexamined assumptions" and an "almost willful blindness" on the part of the critics. Robinson concluded that the entire New Testament was written before the destruction of the temple in AD 70. I would largely agree with him on this matter, except to say that there is good evidence in the writings of the church fathers that the book of Revelation was written near the end of Domitian's reign, around AD 95.

27. For more on the dating of the New Testament, go to the link "Bible" at AlwaysBeReady.com and see "When Was the New Testament Completed?"

28. See the Qur'an, Surah 19:30-35. Regarding this popular notion that Jesus was only a good teacher, see the C.S. Lewis quote at the end of question 8.

29. Regarding the prophecies Jesus fulfilled, see Luke 24:25-27; John 5:46; Acts 3:18. (For a partial list of Old Testament prophecies that Jesus fulfilled, go to the link "Jesus Christ" at AlwaysBeReady.com). Regarding Jesus' sinless life, see John 8:46; Hebrews 4:15. Regarding His miracles, see Mark

2:10-12; John 10:36-38. Regarding His resurrection, see John
2:18-22; Romans 1:4.

30. According to Buddhist tradition, Buddha's imperfections
required him to live more than a hundred thousand past lives
working off his karma and building up the perfections that
he needed to finally become a Buddha like others who had
achieved that state before him. Concerning Muhammad,
we are told that he cried out, "O Allah! Set me apart from
my sins as the East and West are set apart from each other
and clean me from sins as a white garment is cleaned of dirt.
O Allah! Wash off my sins with water, snow and hail" (the
Hadith, vol. 1, bk. 12, no. 711, narrated by Abu Huraira). In
addition to the Hadith, the Qur'an also identifies Muhammad as a sinner. See Surah 40:55, 48:2, and 47:19.

31. Some of the evidences for Christ's resurrection are discussed
in question 19.

32. When I talk to people who have chosen a homosexual life-
style, I rarely even bring up their sexual preference. I use
God's law—the Ten Commandments—when witnessing
to homosexuals. The Bible tells us that the law was made for
homosexuals. First Timothy 1:8-11 says, "But we know that
the law is good if one uses it lawfully, knowing this: that the
law is not made for a righteous person, but for the lawless
and insubordinate, for the ungodly and for sinners, for the
unholy and profane, for murderers of fathers and murderers
of mothers, for manslayers, for fornicators, for sodomites [the
NASB translates this word as "homosexuals"], for kidnappers,
for liars, for perjurers, and if there is any other thing that is

contrary to sound doctrine, according to the glorious gospel of the blessed God which was committed to my trust." If you use the law when you witness to homosexuals, you will not even have to touch on their sexual preference and risk being accused of hating homosexuals. The law will show the homosexual that he is guilty of numerous other sins. When the homosexual turns to God, puts his faith in Jesus, and is born again, God will give him a new heart with new desires (Ezekiel 36:25-27; 2 Corinthians 5:17; Ephesians 4:22-24). This approach with homosexuals is something I gleaned from Ray Comfort (see his website at www.livingwaters.com).

33. Stephen (Acts 7:59-60) was the first of many of the early church's martyrs. See *Foxe's Book of Martyrs* by John Foxe (1516–1587) to read how the original disciples and others were persecuted and killed. This book, which is in the public domain, can be found online.

34. For a long list of scientists with Ph.D.s from prestigious institutions who are skeptical of the Darwinian theory of evolution, see www.DissentFromDarwin.org.

35. The first quote is from an interview with Dr. Gary Habermas at www.biola.edu/antonyflew. The second quote was taken from www.aim.org/aim-column/former-atheist-says-god-exists. Accessed on June 15, 2009. Antony Flew explains why he changed his mind in his book *There Is a God: How the World's Most Notorious Atheist Changed His Mind* (HarperOne, 2007).

36. For an excellent treatment of this topic see Michael Behe's book *Darwin's Black Box* (The Free Press, 1996).

37. J.Y.T. Greig, ed., *The Letters of David Hume* (Clarendon Press, 1932), 1:187.

38. For more on this topic of God's existence, go to the link "God, Evidence for" at AlwaysBeReady.com.

39. When we speak of God being omnipotent, or all-powerful, we are affirming that God can do whatever is possible to do. It is impossible for God to do things contrary to His unchanging nature. For example, God cannot lie (Titus 1:2), He cannot be tempted by evil (James 1:13), and He cannot cease to exist (Psalm 90:2).

40. Here is the dilemma. Genesis 4 says that Adam and Eve had three boys, Cain, Abel and Seth. Then it says in Genesis 4:17 that Cain knew his wife, and she conceived a child named Enoch. "Well," the skeptic asks, "if Adam and Eve were the first people God made, where in the world did Cain get his wife?"

41. Support for the 1446 BC date of the Exodus from Egypt, followed shortly by the giving of the law to Moses, "comes from the biblical record and archeological evidence. First, in 1 Kings 6:1 the time between the Exodus and the beginning of Solomon's temple construction (in the fourth year of his reign) was 480 years. Since the fourth year of Solomon's reign was 966 BC, the Exodus was in 1446. Also in the time of Jephthah (ca. 1100 BC) Israel had been in the land for 300 years (Judges 11:26). Therefore 300 years plus the 40 years of the wilderness sojourn and some time to conquer Heshbon places the Exodus in the middle of the

15th century." (*Bible Knowledge Commentary, Old Testament,* Cook Communications Ministries, 2000).

Jim Tetlow writes, "To marry near of kin in the ancient world was common. Yet, beginning about 1500 BC, God forbid this practice. The reason is simple—the genetic mutations (resulting from the curse) had a cumulative effect. Though Cain could safely marry his sister because the genetic pool was still relatively pure at that time, by Moses' day the genetic errors had swelled. Today, geneticists confirm that the risk of passing on a genetic abnormality to your child is much greater if you marry a close relative because relatives are more likely to carry the same defective gene. If they procreate, their offspring are more apt to have this defect expressed." (*101 Scientific Facts and Foreknowledge,* Eternal Productions, 2005, number 48).

42. See 1 Peter 3:15; 2 Timothy 2:24-26.

43. This paragraph is largely adapted from Norman Geisler and Frank Turek, *I Don't Have Enough Faith to Be an Atheist* (Crossway, 2004), p. 312. For more help on the alleged parallels between ancient pagan religions and Christianity, click on "Zeitgeist" at AlwaysBeReady.com. *Zeitgeist* is the name of an online video that is repopularizing this question. In this video, Peter Joseph, the writer and director, seeks to persuade his viewers that the authors of the New Testament borrowed the idea of Jesus' virgin birth, December 25 birth date, 12 disciples, miracles, crucifixion, and resurrection from astrological sources and ancient pagan mystery religions that were around long before the time of

Christ. Many of the charges put forth in *Zeitgeist* are based on outdated, disproved ideas that were in circulation at the beginning of the last century. Here are some examples of the errors in the video.

First, *Zeitgeist* states that Attis (a Roman deity) was crucified, dead for three days, and then resurrected. This is absolutely not true to the mythological account. In the mythological story, Attis was unfaithful to his goddess lover, and in a jealous rage she made him insane. In that insanity, Attis castrated himself and fled into the forest, where he bled to death. As J. Gresham Machen points out, "The myth contains no account of a resurrection; all that Cybele [the Great Mother goddess] is able to obtain is that the body of Attis should be preserved, that his hair should continue to grow, and that his little finger should move." *Zeitgeist's* claims that Attis was crucified and resurrected are not only inaccurate but very misleading. And that is just the tip of the iceberg. The alleged resurrection of Attis isn't even mentioned until after AD 150, long after the time of Jesus.

Second, *Zeitgeist* claims that Christianity borrowed the idea of three kings for its nativity story from ancient religions. Of course, this is outrageous. The Bible knows nothing of three kings showing up after Jesus' birth. Three kings is an idea that occasionally appears on some poorly researched Christmas cards, but not in the Bible. Matthew's Gospel simply says,

"Now after Jesus was born in Bethlehem of Judea in the days of Herod the king, behold, wise men from the East came to Jerusalem" (Matthew 2:1). The wise men (or *magi*) were not kings, and the Bible does not mention their number. During the Middle Ages, a legend developed that the magi were three kings, but this is purely legend, not something taught in the Scriptures.

Third, *Zeitgeist* claims that the authors of the New Testament borrowed the December 25 date for Jesus' birth from ancient pagan sources. Again, this is ridiculous. Where in the New Testament do we read of *any* date associated with the birth of Jesus? Nowhere! We have no idea when Jesus was born. The December 25 date originated long after the Gospels were written. Professor Edwin Yamauchi explains that not until about AD 336 did December 25 become the official date to celebrate Jesus' birth. The sheer absence of any date in the New Testament documents is sufficient to overturn *Zeitgeist's* claim. Yamauchi's explanation further demonstrates its audacity.

44. Some accounts say 1841, others say 1842. *The Encyclopedia Britannica* says, "Before Richard Owen introduced the term *Dinosauria* in 1842, there was no concept of anything even like a dinosaur" (*Encyclopedia Britannica 2004 Ultimate Reference Suite DVD,* s.v. "dinosaur").

45. See teacher.scholastic.com/researchtools/articlearchives/dinos/dinobaby.htm. Accessed on October 11, 2005.

46. "Although there are about 668 names of dinosaurs, there are perhaps only 55 different 'kinds' of dinosaurs" (www.answersingenesis.org/docs2/4351news7-26-2000.asp). Accessed on October 11, 2005.

47. "According to Genesis 6:15, the Ark measured 300 x 50 x 30 cubits, which is about 460 x 75 x 44 feet, with a volume of 1.54 million cubic feet. Researchers have shown that this is the equivalent volume of 522 standard railroad stock cars (US), each of which can hold 240 sheep. By the way, only 11% of all land animals are larger than a sheep." (www.answersingenesis .org/docs2/4351news7-26-2000.asp). Accessed on October 11, 2005. For a thoroughly researched book that answers just about every conceivable question or attack on the feasibility of Noah's Ark, I highly recommend John Woodmorappe, *Noah's Ark: A Feasibility Study* (Institute for Creation Research, 1996).

48. See Henry M. Morris, *Science and the Bible, Revised and Expanded* (Moody Press, 1986), p. 77.

49. I drew much of my answer for this question from information provided by Answers In Genesis. See their website at www.answersingenesis.org.

50. See Surahs 112:1-4 and 4:48 in the Qur'an.

51. For example, Surah 2:276 says, "Allah does not love any ungrateful sinner." Surah 3:32 says, "Surely Allah does not love the unbelievers." Surah 4:36 says, "Surely Allah does not love him who is proud." Surah 6:141 says, "Surely He does not love the extravagant."

52. For a great insider's look at Muslim life and beliefs by two former Muslims who are now committed Christians, see Ergun and Emir Caner, *Unveiling Islam* (Kregel, 2002).

53. For a more in-depth look at Islam, go to the link "Islam" at AlwaysBeReady.com. Another excellent resource is Norman

ONE-MINUTE ANSWERS TO SKEPTICS

Geisler and Abdul Saleeb, *Answering Islam: The Crescent in Light of the Cross* (Baker Books, 2002).

54. The Bible spoke accurately about the sun some 1500 years before Muhammad was born, saying of the sun, "Its rising is from one end of heaven, and its circuit to the other end" (Psalm 19:6).

55. Here are just a couple of examples. The Qur'an teaches that Noah and all of his family survived the flood (Surah 21:76) but also states that one of Noah's sons drowned (Surah 11:42-43). The Qur'an states that Pharaoh drowned (Surah 28:40; 17:103; 43:55) but also says that he survived (Surah 10:90-92). For more examples of contradictions in the Qur'an, click on "Islam" at AlwaysBeReady.com.

56. Here are four examples.

- The Bible says there was darkness for three hours while Jesus was on the cross (Matthew 27:45; Mark 15:33; Luke 23:44). According to a Book of Mormon prophecy (Helaman 14:27), at the time of Christ's crucifixion, "darkness should cover the face of the whole earth for the space of three days."

- The Bible says that Jesus was born in the town of Bethlehem (Luke 2:4; Micah 5:2). According to the Book of Mormon, Jesus was born in Jerusalem (Alma 7:10).

- The Bible says believers were first called Christians after Paul's ministry in Antioch (Acts 11:26). The Book of Mormon claims people were known by this title as early as 73 BC (Alma 46:15).

- In the Old Testament, the only ones who could be priests were the descendants of Levi, one of the 12 sons of Israel (Numbers 3:9-10). The Book of Mormon claims that descendants of the tribe of Manasseh were made priests (Alma 10:3; 2 Nephi 5:26).

The Book of Mormon has many of these kinds of contradictions. For more examples, see www.irr.org and www.utlm.org.

57. Speaking of the Jews, the Book of Mormon prophesies in 2 Nephi 10:7, "But behold, thus saith the Lord God: When the day cometh that they shall believe in me, that I am Christ, then have I covenanted with their fathers that they shall be restored in the flesh, upon the earth, unto the lands of their inheritance." According to the Book of Mormon, God prophesies that the Jews would be restored to their land, but only when they would acknowledge Jesus as God. Well, the Jews are back in their land today, but who would suggest that it happened as a result of their having believed that Jesus was God? That certainly was not the case. According to Deuteronomy 18:20-22, God's prophets had to be correct 100 percent of the time. The Book of Mormon has failed the test. To see some of Joseph Smith's false prophecies, see www.utlm.org/onlineresources/falseprophecies.htm.

58. Joseph Smith himself said that the golden plates, from which he supposedly got the Book of Mormon, were translated letter-by-letter and "by the power of God" (*History of the Church,* i, pp. 54-55) and that the Book of Mormon was "the most correct of any book on earth" (*History of the Church,*

4:461; this is also stated in the introduction of the Book of Mormon). If that were true, there should not have been a need for any corrections—even spelling and grammatical errors. But, there have been changes. Lots of them. In fact, there have been more than 4000 changes made to the Book of Mormon between the time the original was published in 1830 and the current edition published in 1981 (Ron Rhodes and Marian Bodine, *Reasoning from the Scriptures with the Mormons,* Harvest House, 1995, p. 117). Many of the changes were corrections to Joseph Smith's misspellings and grammatical errors, but there have been many more changes that are quite substantial. For example, 1 Nephi 11:21 says (in the 1830 edition) that Jesus is "the eternal *Father.*" Today's version says (in the same verse) that Jesus is: "the *son* of the eternal Father." Go to www.utlm.org/onlinebooks/3913intro .htm to see numerous other examples. To see scanned pages of the original 1830 version of the Book of Mormon, go to www.irr.org.

59. As you know, to plagiarize is to take ideas or writings from another and offer them as one's own. The Book of Mormon does this hundreds of times. It puts forth some 27,000 words that were taken directly from the King James Version of the Bible (Ron Rhodes and Marian Bodine, *Reasoning from the Scriptures with the Mormons,* p. 121). There are even whole chapters lifted right out of the King James Version. In fact, even the italicized words in the King James Version have been plagiarized. The italicized words, as noted in the preface of the King James Version, were added by the King James translators to add clarity. And yet, even those words ended up in the Book of Mormon! If, as Joseph Smith says,

the golden plates he supposedly translated, were originally penned between 600 BC and AD 421, how could the Book of Mormon contain such extensive quotations from the King James Version of the Bible, which was written in English and wasn't even published until 1611 (more than 1000 years later)? That is a question the Mormon Church does not like to be asked.

60. The Book of Mormon tells us of two different nations that supposedly once existed in North America: the Nephite and Lamanite nations. We are told in the Book of Mormon that these nations had huge populations who lived in large, fortified cities. They allegedly waged large-scale wars with each other for hundreds of years, in which hundreds of thousands of people were killed. The final battle was in AD 385 near Hill Cumorah in present-day New York State (see Mormon 6:9-15 in the Book of Mormon). Yet despite these huge populations, cities, and wars, archaeologists have not been able to discover a single thing that would indicate that these people groups ever existed or that these events actually ever occurred. Dave Hunt writes, "Not one piece of evidence has ever been found to support the Book of Mormon—not a trace of the large cities it names, no ruins, no coins, no letters or documents or monuments, nothing in writing. Not even one of the rivers or mountains or any of the topography it mentions has ever been identified" (*In Defense of the Faith,* Harvest House, 1996, p. 156). This has been verified by the Smithsonian Institute in Washington DC, which stated in 1980, "The Smithsonian Institution has never used The Book of Mormon in any way as a scientific guide. Smithsonian archaeologists see no direct connection

ONE-MINUTE ANSWERS TO SKEPTICS

between the archaeology of the New World and the subject matter of the book." *National Geographic* magazine stated in 1990 that "there is no archaeological evidence to verify the history of early peoples of the Western Hemisphere as presented in the Book of Mormon." On August 12, 1998, the National Geographic Society stated, "Archaeologists and other scholars have long probed the hemisphere's past, and the Society does not know of anything found so far that has substantiated the Book of Mormon." If Mormons tell you that archaeological evidence does exist, put the burden of proof on them. Ask for documentation from non-Mormon sources that you can examine.

61. Dr. Thomas Key, *The Book of Mormon in the Light of Science* (Utah Missions, 2004). This book documents numerous problems in the Book of Mormon related to archaeology, astronomy, botany, chemistry, geography, geology, history, linguistics, math, microbiology, physics, and zoology. You can download a free copy of this book at tdkey.com.

62. Orson Pratt, *Orson Pratt's Works: On the Doctrines of the Gospel,* "Divine Authenticity of the Book of Mormon" (Deseret News Press, 1851), pp. 1-2.

63. See questions 33 and 34, which also address issues related to Islam.

64. First Samuel 16:7 says, "Man looks at the outward appearance, but the LORD looks at the heart."

About the Author

Charlie Campbell is the director of the Always Be Ready apologetics ministry and a popular guest teacher at churches around the United States, speaking regularly to adults and teenagers on a wide variety of issues related to the defense of the Christian faith. Prior to his current role, he served as a pastor and the director of the School of Ministry at Calvary Chapel in Vista, California, where he taught courses on systematic theology, apologetics, world religions, cults, eschatology, hermeneutics, homiletics and evangelism (1997–2006). He resides in Southern California with his wife and five children.

Booking Information

If you would like to inquire about having Charlie Campbell teach at your church, conference, youth group, retreat, or school, please contact him at info@Always BeReady.com or visit www.AlwaysBeReady.com and click "Contact."

More Helpful Apologetics Books
from Harvest House...

CONVERSATIONAL EVANGELISM
Norman Geisler and David Geisler

This refreshing resource explores how witnessing today involves pre-evangelism through conversation and relationship. You'll discover ways to identify the barriers to belief in order to build a bridge to truth, keep dialogue going with different personality types, and effectively share Christ through open communication and compassion.

CONVICTION WITHOUT COMPROMISE
Norman Geisler and Ron Rhodes

In this remarkably clear presentation, apologetics experts Norman Geisler and Ron Rhodes explore key doctrines in light of the well-known saying "In essentials, unity; in nonessentials, liberty; in all things, charity." Covering 14 essential doctrines and many nonessentials, the authors also provide important instructions for learning to "disagree agreeably."

Commonly Misunderstood Bible Verses
Ron Rhodes

The instruction and wonder of the Bible can be clouded if you're uncertain about the meaning of some verses. Bible scholar and popular author Ron Rhodes empowers you with knowledge and reveals how to interpret Scripture, address common stumbling blocks, and become familiar with and confident in God's message.

Taking a Stand for the Bible
John Ankerberg and Dillon Burroughs

Many so-called experts today are spreading inaccurate or biased information about the Bible. *Taking a Stand for the Bible* helps set the record straight and includes interviews with top Bible scholars who affirm the Bible's integrity and reliability.